Edward S Parkinson

Wonderland

Twelve Weeks in and out of the United States

Edward S Parkinson

Wonderland
Twelve Weeks in and out of the United States

ISBN/EAN: 9783744670777

Printed in Europe, USA, Canada, Australia, Japan

Cover: Foto ©Andreas Hilbeck / pixelio.de

More available books at **www.hansebooks.com**

Our Party Taking it Cool at Muir Glacier.

WONDERLAND;

OR,

TWELVE WEEKS

IN AND OUT OF THE UNITED STATES.

BRIEF ACCOUNT OF

A TRIP ACROSS THE CONTINENT—SHORT RUN INTO MEXICO RIDE
TO THE YOSEMITE VALLEY—STEAMER VOYAGE TO ALASKA.
THE LAND OF GLACIERS VISIT TO THE GREAT SHO-
SHONE FALLS AND A STAGE RIDE THROUGH
THE YELLOWSTONE NATIONAL PARK.

·BY

EDWARD S. PARKINSON.

TRENTON, N. J
MacCrellish & Quigley, Book and Job Printers.

1894

TO

MY FRIENDS AND FELLOW-PASSENGERS

OF

P. R. R. GOLDEN GATE TOUR NUMBER FOUR,

1892,

THIS BOOK IS RESPECTFULLY DEDICATED.

EDWARD S. PARKINSON.

Ḥow I Game to Ẅrite a Book.

Ever since leaving the West, the writer has from time to time acted as correspondent for one of the weekly papers of his native town, and in several instances has been employed on the staff of one of the daily papers of the city of his adoption. He should, therefore, be pardoned for intensified literary ambitions when confronted by allurements of travel so tempting as those presented to him on a leisurely trip of nineteen thousand miles through picturesque America.

The somewhat protracted journey and saunterings, which commenced at New Jersey's capital and extended to the Golden Gate and thence to Alaska, of which this book is briefly descriptive, occurred in the spring and summer of 1892, and occupied a period of three memorable months. Hence the author is constrained to the use of "Twelve Weeks In and Out of the United States" as a fitting title to a narrative whose details will possess the merit of truthfulness if, unhappily, they shall fail in interest.

In addition and incidental to the trip from ocean to ocean, our party crossed the line into Mexico, traversed the Pacific coast States from San Diego to Tacoma, from which point we embarked, *via* British Columbia, for Alaska.

On the return trip we visited the great Sho-shone Falls, Yellowstone Park (appropriately named "Wonderland"), and numerous other points of interest, which are herein described.

While taking frequent notes on the steamer during the Alaska trip the writer was persistently solicited by his fellow-passengers to preserve the record, whether it be printed in book, newspaper or pamphlet form, and forward the same to them as a reminder of scenes and incidents witnessed but once in a life-time. This, therefore, is a further incentive to my more or less willing pen.

The illustrations herein were made from photographs taken by Tabor, of San Francisco ; M. M. Hazeltine, of Baker City, Oregon ; and from Kodak views taken by Miss Serrill, of Philadelphia—to each of whom the writer hereby expresses appreciation. The Pennsylvania Railroad Company and Union Pacific Railroad Company also kindly loaned some cuts, which add much to the completeness of the book.

If the following pages shall prove of interest to such proportion of the large army of American tourists as shall read them, or be in any degree helpful to them in making a similar journey, the author's efforts will have been amply rewarded, and his justification for having "written a book" will be complete.

TRENTON, N. J.,   E. S. P.
    July, 15, 1893.

INDEX.

ILLUSTRATIONS.

WONDERLAND

OR

TWELVE WEEKS IN AND OUT OF THE UNITED STATES.

* * * *

CHAPTER I.

WESTWARD BOUND.

THE blustering weather of a New Jersey March was upon us. Streets and pavements were swept on alternate days by gusts of rain and clouds of dust. Trees, lawns and all out-doors still wore a look of wintry dilapidation, and even pedestrians cut awkward figures attempting to round corners, cross streets or enter doorways in the face of the searching winds which whistled in doleful tones around the corners of houses and down chimney-flues, bringing to vivid realization the discomfort attending the traditional "lingering of Spring in the lap of Winter."

While enjoying the comforts of our home and watching an occasional pedestrian struggling

2

against the driving wind, our thoughts turned to pictures of the "Sunny South," where a few years since we had, on a visit to Florida, exchanged the ill-tempered March weather of New Jersey for the balmy atmosphere of that land of oranges and palm-trees.

Conversation became animated as little by little the ladies of the household pointed out the comforts and delights of that more congenial clime and dwelt on the absence of intrusive chills and dust and the exhilaration of a change from the cyclonic winds now roaring in the chimney to the placidity of a zephyr in the land of alligators.

Such comparisons proved too convincing as from day to day they were adverted to, and soon it was decided to arrange for a journey.

"If we were only in California," remarked the most enthusiastic of our group, "all this disagreeable weather would be avoided, and we could there choose between the comforts of easy-chairs on a hotel piazza in mellow sunshine, and the more active contact with Nature in orange groves and on grassy lawns, where breezes fan but do not ruffle, and where the balmy atmosphere imparts a feeling of comfort and healthfulness quite the reverse of that which we now experience."

As all agreed that there was nothing apparent to prevent the real consummation of a hope so ardently expressed, it required but a short time to outline the journey and perfect the plans for a three months' tour.

It was a beautiful morning when we boarded the "Golden Gate" special, at Trenton, and began our trans continental trip. The train was composed entirely of Pullman cars, five in number. The first was occupied as a baggage-car, barber shop, bath room and smoker; the second as a dining-car; the third and fourth, sleepers; and the fifth a combination parlor, library and observation-car. All were of the latest pattern and lighted throughout with electricity. The parlor was furnished with rattan furniture, and on one side was an upright piano of the best make. In short, we were traveling in a modern hotel on wheels.

Our party, according to the directory issued by the railroad company, consisted of twenty-eight persons, most of whom resided in or near Philadelphia. When the train arrived at the City of Brotherly Love the greater part of the company came on board, and we then began our journey toward the great West. The suburban towns, with their neat stations, were passed in rapid succession. All through the Chester Valley, the garden spot of Pennsylvania, the thrifty farmers were busy tilling the ground preparatory to planting their tobacco crop, for which this region is famous. Short stops were made at Lancaster and Harrisburg.

At Altoona an extra engine was attached to the train to help us over the mountains. The wonderful Horseshoe Curve was passed in a drizzling rain, but that did not deter many from taking seats in the observation-car, where they could obtain an unobstructed view of it.

Twelve miles west of Altoona the train entered the tunnel which penetrates the Alleghany mountains and marks the highest elevation of the Pennsylvania Railroad system. Emerging from the tunnel the train passed Galitzen, a town named after Count Galitzen, a Russian Nobleman who renounced the pomp and glory of the Russian court and became a Roman Catholic priest. He settled in this section long before the railroad was constructed, and built up around him a settlement which at one time did not have a Protestant within its borders. His remains now rest in a vault in the grounds of the convent at Loretta, a small village near Cresson. Here the extra engine was dispensed with and the train commenced the descent of the western slope of the Alleghany mountains. In a few moments we whirled past Cresson, a summer

Interior of Dining Car.

resort under the control of the Pennsylvania Railroad Company. The Mountain House and cottages were in full view of the train, and the

well-kept lawns indicated a very attractive place.
In a short time the train passed ill-fated Johns-
town, where but recently hundreds of lives and
millions of dollars in property were lost by the
bursting of the dam which confined the waters of
the South Fork, then owned and used as a rendezvous by the South Fork Fishing Club.

The sun had disappeared in the west when we
entered the coke region. The lurid flames which
shot up from the numerous ovens made a sight
readily transformed by a lively imagination into
close relationship to the infernal regions. Further on we entered the domain of natural gas and
saw for the first time the startling beauty of the
burning fluid shooting upward from its mysteri-
ous abode in nature's retorts. As we approached
Pittsburg the lights from the furnaces of the
Edgar Thompson and Carnagie Iron and Steel
Works illumined the heavens for miles around.
Night was full upon us when the train entered
this city, where only a short stop was made.
Here our party was augmented by the arrival of
four ladies, who, as soon as they had arranged
their packages in their state-rooms, joined the
others in the parlor-car.

The evening was passed in getting acquainted,
and before retiring we were as much at ease as

though we had known each other for years instead of a few hours. With the exception of three persons, who were traveling for their health, the entire party was on pleasure bent.

Pleasantly passed the hours until, by way of diversion, a rather pretty but over-confident young lady from Boston betook herself to the piano and showered solos of such distressful melody upon all present that, in self-defence, our party could do nothing so appropriate as to retire for the night. The day had brought us many delights, and we had withstood the fatigue of climbing the Alleghany mountains, and even absorbed much natural gas *en route*, but not until the Boston singer appeared at the piano had we realized a fitting sense of weariness.

On awaking in the morning we were in the northern part of Indiana, and by ten o'clock we arrived at Chicago, one hour and a half ahead of schedule time.

At the station a number of carriages were waiting to take us sight-seeing through the resident portion of the city and the different parks. Being still early in the season, very few of the lawns in front of the residences had been stripped of their winter garb. As we were near Jackson Park, the driver was told to take us to the Exposition grounds. After paying the admittance fee of twenty-five cents, we drove into the grounds, where a large army of workmen and artisans were busy constructing the different buildings for the World's Fair. The women's building was the only one yet completed. Luncheon was served at the Auditorium Hotel, the dining room of which is on the ninth floor, and from our table an excellent view of Lake Michigan could be had. Most of the afternoon was spent in visiting the large business houses, and at the jewelry stores almost every one of the party bought souvenir spoons of the Windy City.

Reaching the station sometime before the departure of our train, two eager tourists engaged a carriage to take them through the tunnels under the Chicago river. Entering the shaky rig, they were quickly off and soon arrived at the opening which leads under the river. Waiting for a moment until a car had passed, the driver urged his horse to a gallop. Before reaching the middle of the tunnel another car was heard approaching in the rear, clanging its bell at a furious rate. The driver applied the whip to his already galloping old steed, which looked ready to drop at every jump, and the top of the incline was reached just ahead of the car. One of the occupants, a lady, was considerably frightened, but had the courage to say not a word until safely off the car tracks, when she vowed that she would not soon again be guilty of another such "wild-goose chase" At five o'clock all were again on board the train, bound westward

It was early in the morning when we crossed the Missouri river and entered Nebraska. After a short stop in Omaha, to change engines, the train continued on its flight toward the Pacific. Soon we were out on the broad and undulating prairies. For miles we could see the smoke arising from the burning straw stacks which the farmers were destroying preparatory to plowing for the spring planting. As the train sped farther and farther west, an occasional "sod house" would appear, and before the sun went down few farm-houses were seen that were not built of sod. The towns and cities, however, showed a far more progressive spirit than many Eastern towns of five or six times the number of inhabitants. Every town of over 2,500 inhabitants was lighted with electricity, and many of them had electric railways.

Our trip across this wonderful State was made more pleasant because of the recent rains which had thoroughly soaked the ground and settled the dust.   In the evening a progressive-euchre party was organized, and it was late before the players retired.

On awaking in the morning we were in the yards near the Union depot, in Denver.   After breakfast carriages were called and a tour of inspection of this model Western city was made. The magnificent homes in the resident portion were particularly striking.   It seemed as if a different architect had planned each house, and that all had put forth an especial effort to make a comfortable home, with a pleasing perspective.

Denver is one of the most progressive cities in the West.   Great fortunes have been (and are still being) made in real estate.   I had the pleasure of meeting General Lessig, who settled in Denver when there were only 3,000 inhabitants, and who went there with a very small capital.   He invested in real estate and is now several times a millionaire.   One piece of property in particular was bought by him at a cost of $1,500, and was sold recently for $135,000.   The present owners hold it at $250,000.

The streets are well shaded except in the

business portion of the city. Along each side-walk runs an irrigating ditch; into this the water is turned every day in order to supply moisture to the trees, without which they would die, as the air is very dry and rain seldom falls.

The business houses, although not so high as those in Chicago, are fully as handsome, and rent for fabulous sums.

At the conclusion of our ride we were taken to the Windsor Hotel, where luncheon was prepared for the entire company. As the after-noon was left to our own disposal, many of the photograph-galleries and curio-stores were visited. As usual, almost every one had a col-lection of souvenir spoons to show to the com-pany on returning to the car.

While walking through one of the streets I had the fortune to meet an old schoolmate, who had "gone west" to grow up with the country. It was one of those pleasing episodes which sometimes startle a traveler when far from home and least expecting it. He was particularly enthusiastic over the growth of Denver, pre-dicted for it a glorious future, and gave con-vincing reasons for his unbounded faith.

Bidding farewell to the "Queen City of the Plains," as Denver is popularly known in the

West, our train started for Colorado Springs,
celebrated as a haven for people of weak lungs
and delicate constitutions. Many of Denver's
citizens make it their summer resort, and
thus also escape the hot winds from the
plains. It was soon noticed that two of our
fellow-passengers were not in their accustomed
places, and upon inquiry it was ascertained that
one of the young ladies had been taken suddenly ill, and was unable to leave the hotel.
Her mother had remained with her, but they
fully expected to proceed on their journey in a
few days, and, if possible, meet us at Salt Lake
City.   .

The road winds through the foot-hills, gradually ascending until an altitude of 7,238 feet
above tide water is reached. The scenery is
enchanting. On many of the hills are formations known as Spanish castles, and looking
from the platform of the observation-car one
could readily imagine that he was traveling in
Spain and actually gazing upon her ancient
ruins. Standing out by itself, thus making it
more prominent, is a mountain surmounted by a
rock of very large dimensions, known as Castle
Rock. It is a wonderful curiosity, and looks as
if it had been chiseled by the hand of man

instead of the quiet but powerful work of air and moisture.

All along we could see the irrigating-ditches which carry water from the mountains and distribute it to the different ranches and towns in the valley. The land lying below these ditches is cultivated and makes large returns, while that above is used for grazing purposes. The Yucca, or soap-weed, grows in great quantities above these ditches. It resembles the century-plant very much, though the leaves are somewhat smaller. The root of this plant was once the only soap used by the Indians and Mexicans, who pulverized it and used it in the same manner as people of this day use the numerous powdered soap compounds.

Palmer Lake was the highest point reached. It is an artificial body of water formed by damming a mountain stream. In the centre of it is a fountain throwing a jet of water fully twenty-five feet into the air. The train stopped for a few moments at the station, and while the engineer was overlooking his engine two irrepressible tramps came up to the cars begging—thus demonstrating that his species is universal and beyond the possibility of reform or suppression, even in the highest altitudes of the Rocky mountains.

The down-trip of the train was rendered very pleasant by General Lessig, who entertained the whole party with reminiscences of his life in the West. He has been in Colorado since 1867, and has seen the State grow from an insignificant Territory to one of the richest and most progressive States in the Union.

It was late in the evening when we reached Colorado Springs, and after a hearty supper at the Antlers, most of us retired. A number attended a ball given in honor of the company.

Sunday was a day of rest, excepting a walk to the South Cañon of the Cheyenne. On the way we passed a stand where broncos were for hire, and as one of our party, who had already gained a reputation for seeing a little more and going a little farther than anybody else, was desirous of taking "a ride," a bargain was struck and he was soon astride one of the animals. This particular bronco had formerly been used as a packer on the Pike's Peak trail, and had acquired a very slow gait, which no amount of coaxing or pounding could get him to abandon. Another peculiarity of this Rocky mountain pet was that he would never cross a ditch first, so every stream our equestrian friend came to he had to dismount and lead the bronco

across, then remount and be off on a very slow
walk. On returning, our rider got off to lead
him over the stream, when, to his surprise, he
started on a trot for the tie-post, where he meekly
stood with a lazy expression in his eyes which
indicated that he would breathe his life out
sweetly there rather than carry a tenderfoot
another yard. That bronco is probably standing there yet.

In the afternoon we walked up the cañon to
the Seven Falls. On all sides the cliffs were
almost perpendicular to heights of 1,000 and
1,500 feet, and at some points we seemed cut
off from communication with the outer world.
Every movement forward brought another surprise, and when the view of the Seven Falls
burst upon us we stood in utter astonishment for
several minutes. We then ascended the stairs
that run alongside the falls. It was a tiresome
climb of two hundred and sixty steps, but every
step was repaid. At the top of the falls a trail
leads to the grave of Helen Hunt Jackson,
author of "Ramona." Her body no longer
rests in this romantic spot, but the different
stones left there by admirers of her works still
remain, although every visitor now takes a small
stone away as a memento.

The Seven Falls.

Monday morning, a carriage having been engaged, we were off bright and early to visit the famous springs of Manitou and the Garden of the Gods.

Manitou is about five miles from Colorado Springs, and is connected with the latter by an electric railway. The wagon road between the two resorts is in very good condition, making the drive a pleasant one. About midway between the two cities lies Colorado City, the first capital of the Silver State. It is now a progressive little village and shows some signs of substantial growth. Rounding a turn in the road, Manitou comes into view. It is nestled in the valley overshadowed by Pike's Peak. As we approached the town we drove past several villas, with their groves of graceful trees and maze of shrubbery. It appears to be composed of hotels, boarding-houses and small shops, where are exposed for sale agates of various kinds, curiosities and Indian work, for which exorbitant prices are obtained.

The springs are six in number, of which the Soda and the Ute Iron are the largest and most popular. At each of these a dipper-boy is kept busy handing out the water. Of course he gets no pay for his work, but he is not unwilling to

3

accept a nickel from every drinker. The owners of these two springs have large pavilions where curiosities and Colorado jewelry are sold at the usual high prices.

After driving through the principal street and going to the Pike's Peak railroad station to see the peculiar engine used for carrying passengers to the summit of the mountain, our driver took us over to Ute Pass, up past a beautiful little waterfall, known as Rainbow Falls, to the entrance of the Manitou caverns. Here all alighted from the carriage, and, after paying a dollar each, a lamp was handed us and we were told to "follow the guide." Passing into a medium-sized chamber we were all asked to stop and deliver our tickets, after which the guide took us through the few remaining rooms. In one of the chambers is seen what is called the "Grand Organ," but it seemed very inharmonious when one of the guides tried to play a familiar tune on it. In the end of one room is a curious collection of bones, said to have been found in the cavern. All of the formations in the cave are small and insignificant when compared with those of Luray and the Grottoes of the Shenandoah.

Retracing our way we pass through Manitou and start for one of the greatest wonders of the West, the "Garden of the Gods."

Entering the Garden we are first attracted to a number of formations known as the Toad Stools, some of which are fully fifteen feet in height. Balanced Rock is then passed. It is an immense boulder poised on a slender base, and looks as if it would fall at the least touch. We are now kept busy listening to the names of the different formations. All animals are shown us, and the imagination readily sees the resemblance. The Quakers, Liberty, Ben Butler and various other formations are passed. All are formed by the combined action of wind, rain, sunbeam and frost, the all-powerful tools of Nature.

As we pass through the Gateway and see the wonderful formation, appearing as if it were hewn through the solid rock, we involuntarily exclaim, "How wonderful are Thy works, O Lord!" It has the appearance of two lofty slabs of red sandstone set opposite each other, about seventy-five feet apart, and rising to a height of about three hundred feet from the road-bed. A little back from the gate, in the Garden, stand the Cathedral Spires. They are of the same kind of sandstone—a brilliant red. It is impossible to describe the wonderful works Nature has displayed in this marvelous "Garden

Gateway, Garden of the Gods.

of the Gods." The different formations can be photographed, but the colorings can never be transferred to canvas.

Passing out of the Garden our drive takes us to Glen Eyrie, the home of General Palmer. It is a garden on a smaller scale, although some of the formations are even more remarkable than those in the Garden of the Gods. One rock, known as "Major Domo," rises to a height of three hundred feet, and because of a curious formation on top looks as if it would fall without warning.

Leaving the Glen we are taken to the Antlers, where a lunch is in readiness.

Before repairing to our hotel on wheels we bade good-bye to three of our company. Two of them had only intended coming this far, while the other, one of the Pittsburg contingent, had expected to go to the Pacific Slope. It was upon the recommendation of a physician that she had concluded to return to the East.

Evening found our company again in the cars, glad to get back to the comforts of our home on wheels.

It was quite early in the morning when the jolting of the cars brought the realization that our train had pulled out of the station at Colorado Springs, and that we were again moving toward the Pacific Slope.

We arrived at Pueblo about seven o'clock, and while engines were being changed and various other matters attended to a number of us got off the train and walked through a portion of the town. Pueblo is distinctively a railroad centre, being the division headquarters of the Denver and Rio Grande systems It is also a manufacturing town. A number of smelters have been erected here, and one of the trainmen informed us that fully three fourths of the ore that passed over the Denver and Rio Grande railroad stopped at Pueblo. The Union depot is one of the finest in the West. The railroads that bring the ore from the mines are narrow-gauge, and when a broad gauge road is met an extra rail is put between the two rails, making two tracks on three rails. It seemed very novel at first to see a standard-gauge engine pulling narrow-gauge cars, but this soon wore off. After leaving Pueblo we passed through a section of country where numerous oil-wells had been sunk, and it suggested sights in western Pennsylvania on our first day out.

After passing through the oil country we partook of our morning meal, which the crisp air,

Interior of Observation-Car.

combined with the walk at Pueblo, stimulated
to a full measure of enjoyment. Breakfast over,
all hands hurried to the observation-car in order

to get advantageous seats for viewing the grand
cañon of the Arkansas. As we approached the
cañon the brakeman showed us where three men
had "held up" a train but a short time before.
It seemed a favorable spot for such enterprise,
and a feeling of self preservation ripened a desire
to pass on into less "favorable" territory.

Entering the cañon the railroad skirts along
the banks of the Arkansas river, hugging the
base of the almost perpendicular walls of granite
which rise over one thousand feet above the
river-bed. The narrowest part of the cañon is
known as the "Royal Gorge," and when the
railroad was first projected it was deemed almost
impossible to build it through a cañon where
there appeared to be scarcely room for the river
alone, and where the granite mountains presented their almost impenetrable sides as a
barrier to the engineers who surveyed the line.
Leadville, then the centre of all eyes, and the
greatest carbonate mining camp in the world,
must be reached, and the most direct way was
through this cañon. To build the road-bed
through the gorge required much engineering.
The river, dashing at a furious rate, occupied
all the available space, and the granite walls,
refusing to yield their firm grip, caused the

engineers to build a suspension-bridge over the rushing torrent. The bridge does not cross the river, but is built parallel with it, and is supported by girders and braces which rest on both sides of the stream. Our train was stopped on the bridge, and many of us stepped out upon the girders and almost broke our necks looking up to determine how high the smoothly-polished granite walls extended above us. Several of the party had Kodaks and secured some very fine pictures of the surrounding heights. For miles the train rushed along between these high walls of stone and along the banks of the turbulent Arkansas river, which seemed to resent the intrusion of the railroad upon its boundaries by dashing with great fury against the carefully-built masonry of the road-bed. The engineer blew the whistle of the engine several times, the echo of which startlingly reverberated through the cañon.

At Salida we changed to a narrow-gauge road which runs through the Sangre De Cristo range and over the Marshall Pass. The road winds in and around the mountains, making some wonderfully short curves. Many of them put the Horseshoe Curve on the Pennsylvania railroad far into the shade. At one place, when standing on the rear platform of the car, we could see, down in the valley beneath, the track we had traveled over, and far above us was another over which we were soon to ride. We were courteously treated by the traveling engineer of the road, Mr. Barnes, who came to this country some fifteen years ago. As a proof of the healthfulness of the region through which we were passing he informed us that when he left the East he could bearly tip the beam at 130, but that now his weight was 200 and he was still actively "growing up with the country." He took especial pains to point out places of interest along the road. At several stations only a few deserted buildings were seen, the former inhabitants having moved away. Shirley is a striking example of this desolation, having but one house now standing (a half-demolished building once occupied as a saloon), though at one time it was a lively frontier town of about 200 inhabitants. It was at the end of the railroad, and all supplies for the mines were carried from here on burros over to the camps. It flourished in wild western fashion for about six months, when the railroad was extended to a point beyond; then everybody packed up bed and baggage and moved on to the end of the road. On a little hill just above the station stands a lone pine tree, and under it are neglected mounds which cover the remains of seven men who died with their boots on. They were "hold-ups," horse-thieves and gamblers. The residents of the town concluded one night to rid the community of them, so they were taken into custody, and after a trial were hung and buried underneath the spreading branches of the lone pine tree.

As the train approached the top of the mountain large patches of snow were passed and several snow-sheds covered the track. At the summit the train stopped under a long snow-shed to enable the engineer to test the air-brakes before commencing the descent. While waiting, some of us climbed to the top of an observatory to view the surrounding mountains. The wind was blowing a fearful gale, almost taking away one's breath, so we did not stay long, but hurried back to the warm cars. On the descent, Mr. Barnes pointed out Ouray and Chevenaugh peaks, the two highest of the range. They were named for two of the principal chiefs of the Ute Indians, both of whom were friendly to the white settlers. These peaks were covered with snow and towered high above the surrounding mountains.

After dinner at Sargents, the meal-station, we turned our faces toward Salida. While crossing the highest point of the mountains several of the young ladies came near fainting on account of the high altitude and rarity of the air.   As it was, all of the smelling salts bottles were brought into requisition. Arriving at Salida at supper-time we were happily surprised to see the lady who was to return to the East standing on the platform waiting to receive us. She had con-cluded to risk the trip and had come down from Colorado Springs to rejoin the party.

The evening was spent in playing games of various kinds, until a despatch was received from Denver saying that the young lady whom we had left there was not expected to live, and urging her two sisters to return at once. This information threw a gloom over the party, and the departing sisters, who had been among the most spirited of our company, were greatly missed.

We remained in Salida until two o'clock in the morning, in order to pass through the Eagle river and Grand river cañons by daylight. At five o'clock the train pulled into the station at

Leadville, the greatest carbonate camp in the world. Only a few of the party were up to see the sun rise over the peaks and enjoy a walk in the crisp air. The thermometer stood at fourteen degrees above zero on the station platform.

Leaving Leadville the train began to ascend the Tennessee Pass, the highest point reached by the railroad. Here we were 10,418 feet above tide-water. The ground was covered with snow, and the only signs of life were the huts of the tie-choppers and charcoal-burners. This is the great continental "divide." The waters falling on this range flow into both oceans.

The Mount of the Holy Cross, so named from two gulches that cross each other and in which the snow never melts (thus forming a snow-white cross), was passed, but being entirely covered with snow the form of the cross could not be seen.

After descending the pass and speeding by several towns the train entered Eagle river cañon. The walls are over two thousand feet above the railroad, yet on the cliffs and crags are to be seen the shaft-houses and miners' cabins, where the miners work and live, delving for the precious gold and silver abundantly found there. This cañon contains one of the richest gold mines in Colorado. The rocks are of various colors, and, relieved by the sombre pine, form paintings which pen cannot depict nor artist duplicate.

The cañon of the Grand river was next en·tered. It differs from the other cañons, and presents columns, castles, turrets, towers and statues with all imaginable colorings, every point or curve in the road presenting a new and apparently more wonderful formation.

Our next stop was at Glenwood Springs. It is a beautiful place, and is a health and pleasure resort. The hot sulphur springs are the principal attraction. A company controls them and have erected a very handsome bath house. It is built of red sandstone and finished in hard wood. An immense pool for plunge-bathing has been constructed in the open air. One end of the pool, where the water comes directly from the springs, is steaming hot, while the other end is much cooler, the difference in temperature being caused by the introduction of cold water. Where the springs issue from the ground the steam arises in such quantities that houses have been constructed over them and the steam utilized for vapor baths. As the train stopped for more than two hours, all the gentlemen of

our party hired suits and went into the pool.
That the novel bath was greatly enjoyed goes
without saying.   Within twenty-four hours we
had passed through snow and had bathed in hot-
water pools formed by Nature in the open air.

Leaving Glenwood our train wended its way
between mountains and through valleys until
night put an end to views from the car windows.

On awaking in the morning the train was
skirting along the banks of the river Jordan,
which flows from Utah Lake into Great Salt
Lake.   Before breakfast was finished our train
rolled into the station at Salt Lake City, the
great Mormon capital.   Awaiting us when we
alighted from the train was our cousin, Mr.
Harvey J. Jones.   Having been a resident of
the city for some time, we were enabled by his
guidance to visit many places which no doubt
would have been missed had it not been for him.

Leaving the train we took up our quarters at
the Knutsford, the largest hotel owned by the
Gentiles in the city.   As soon as we were comfortably settled a large tally-ho coach rolled up
to the door and we soon occupied seats on top
of it.   Our driver was a Mormon, who took
great pride in showing the handsome buildings
owned by the people of his own religious faith.

He was the son of Heber C. Kimball, one of the
early leaders of the Church, who, during his
lifetime, was next in authority to Brigham
Young, and who, had the latter died first, would
have succeeded to the presidency of the Mormon
Church.   The first place visited was Temple
Square, where the different buildings connected
with the Mormon services are located.   The
square is enclosed by a stone wall about twelve
feet high.   Within the enclosure the grounds
surrounding the buildings are tastefully laid out
with flowers.   The principal buildings are the
Temple, the Tabernacle and the Assembly Hall.
The latter was the first building erected.   Its
ceiling is frescoed with paintings showing the
different temples in which the Mormons worship
or have worshiped, including the one at Nauvoo,
Illinois.   There are also paintings representing
different scenes which led to the finding of the
Golden Tablets.   The Tabernacle is an immense
building, and within it are held the great con-
ferences of the disciples of the Latter-Day Saints,
as the Mormons call themselves.   The roof is
like a hemisphere, and is called "The Turtle
Back" by the unregenerate Gentiles.   Its acous-
tic properties are perfect, being so constructed
that a whisper uttered at the president's desk

can be heard at the farthest end of the building. The Temple is now completed. President Smith, at the laying of the corner-stone, prophesied that it would be forty years in building, and the faithful were determined that the prophecy should be fulfilled. The forty years expired on the sixth of April, 1893, at which time the great Temple was dedicated with imposing ceremonies. Admission to the stairs leading to the towers was secured by tickets, and most of us climbed to the highest point There are three towers on the front of the building, the central one being surmounted by a figure of heroic size representing Maroni, one of the founders of the Church, with an immense trumpet to be blown on the Resurrection Morn, when he will call all the members of the Church of the Latter-Day Saints of Jesus Christ to everlasting bliss.

The view obtained from our elevated position was one of exceeding beauty. In the distance was seen the Wasatch range of mountains, whose crests are covered with perpetual snows All over the valley were farms and truck gardens under the finest state of cultivation In the distance could be seen Great Salt Lake, the wonderful inland sea of North America The river Jordan, as it flowed from Utah Lake to Great

4

Salt Lake, could be distinctly traced. At our feet was the tithing-yard and the home of Brigham Young.

Descending from our lofty position, we once more took our places on the coach and. were driven past the former residences of Brigham Young and notably that of his once favorite wife Amelia. The latter building is now known as the Gardo House, and is occupied by the Keely Institute for the reformation of drunkards. We were shown the graves of Brigham Young and those of his wives who, with him, have "joined the innumerable caravan." When the Gentiles secured control of the municipal government they compelled the children of the president to remove all bodies excepting those of Brigham Young and his wives from their private burial-ground to a cemetery outside of the city limits. The exception was in deference to the distinguished founder of the city.

Salt Lake City is a beautiful place. The streets are wide, and on each side are handsome rows of trees. Clear streams of water, supplied by irrigating canals, flow on each side of the street to supply moisture to the trees. Many of the residences are very handsome, but in the old part of the city most of the houses are built of adobe or sun-dried brick. The largest business-house is the "Co-op," the shortest way of saying "Zion's Co-operative Mercantile Institution." It is the principal trading-house in the territory, and is under the supervision of the Church. Its branches are to be seen in every Mormon settlement.

Fort Douglas, where are stationed the United States troops, is on one of the hills overlooking the city, and is a great pleasure resort. The music by the military band and the evening drills by the soldiers attract many of the citizens every evening.

Garfield Beach is the great bathing resort, and is reached by the Union Pacific railroad. The pavilions are attractive, and bath-houses and suits may be hired at moderate price by all who wish to take a dip in the briny lake. We spent a very pleasant afternoon in watching the bathers disport themselves in the water.

The evening was passed in visiting stores and buying trinkets and silver spoons to take away with us to recall the pleasant time passed within the borders of the great Mormon city, where even a Jew is called a Gentile.

After a good night's rest we were again on the train. Passing along the shores of the lake,

Pavilion at Garfield Beach, Great Salt Lake.

great flocks of sea-gulls and ducks were seen. At Ogden the train stopped for a short time and the party surrounded two men having badges for delegates to a cattlemen's convention and begged all the badges from them. Leaving Ogden we were soon out on the Great American Desert. The barren plains reflected the rays of the sun and caused us to lower the curtains of the cars to relieve our eyes. Stations were frequently passed where only two buildings were visible One would be occupied by the section-boss and the station-agent, the latter performing the duties of operator, station agent and postmaster; the other would probably be occupied by Chinese laborers employed on the railroad.

Sage-brush and grease-weed comprise the only vegetation that thrives on this desert, although at one station we alighted and picked some very pretty and fragrant flowers.

It was a wearisome day and we were glad when night came, so that we could retire and rest our eyes and prepare for more pleasant scenery on the morrow.

CHAPTER II.

CALIFORNIA.

THE day was fast drawing to a close, and the glare from the bare mountains and white sands of the desert was rapidly passing away when our party gathered in the observation car to discuss events, compare plans and make arrangements for continuing the trip after reaching San Francisco. The evening was pleasantly spent in listening to songs and the music of the piano and mandolin furnished by the employés of the railroad. It was quite late when the last "good-nights" were spoken and all had retired.

On awaking in the morning we were somewhat surprised to see the ground covered with snow and the mountains dressed in stately pine forests. Stopping at Truckee a number of us got off to indulge in "snow-ball" and walk around. At one end of the station some practical joker had improvised a cage from a stray box and painted on it this inscription: "A Large Red Bat Caught in the Red Cañon." On looking between the bars a red brick-bat was seen. The "sell" caused considerable merriment, both among the loungers at the station and the members of our party.

After breakfast each member of the party was presented with a carefully-prepared itinerary of the resorts in California. It was the joint work of Mr. Purdy, the tourist agent, and Mrs. Bender, the chaperon, representing the Pennsylvania Railroad Company. They had been several days in preparing it, and we found it a source of great convenience when visiting the different resorts of the Golden State.

Leaving Truckee the train soon entered a long line of snow-sheds. For forty miles we traveled under this overground tunnel. The longest continual shed was thirty-five miles Through open ings in the sides of the shed, where an occasional board had dropped off, glimpses of Donner Lake were to be had. This lake was named after Captain Donner, who led a party of emigrants across the plains and mountains during the early excitement of the gold fever, which raged in the latter part of the forties. The Donner expedition was among the first to cross the plains, and the hardships and dangers experienced have passed into history. Thirty-four of these pioneers died of starvation on the banks of this lake.

Emerging from the sheds we commenced the descent around the mountains. About the middle of the forenoon we rounded Cape Horn, a bold promontory, where the train seemed ready to topple over into the cañon, twenty-five hundred feet below.

When the road was being constructed, workmen were let down by ropes from the cliffs above and suspended in midair until they could drill and blast away rock sufficient to obtain a foothold. A drizzling rain was falling when we passed this wonderful point, and the view of the valley was very much obscured.

Before noon we were in the valley, amid flowers of every variety. The yellow California poppy was seen everywhere. At one of the stations a number of little boys had armloads of flowers for sale. Two immense bouquets were purchased for twenty cents. They were especially fine, and in the East would have cost from $2.00 to $3.50 each.

It was noon when our train pulled into the station at Sacramento, where a short stop was made to receive orders Most of the party were at lunch, and consequently were unable to leave and see much of the town. The afternoon was spent in rolling through magnificent farms and ranches and breathing an atmosphere fragrant with blooming flowers and alfalfa. Numerous groves of live-oak trees were passed, under which herds of cattle had gathered to enjoy the cool shade of the overspreading boughs.

Arriving at Oakland, where we took the ferry for San Francisco, we left our comfortable cars and departed from the care of the obliging Pennsylvania tourist agent and chaperons To say that we regretted the parting would feebly express it. It was like leaving home to become strangers in a strange land.

Before the boat had fairly left the slip the subject of a trip to "Chinatown" was broached, and by the time San Francisco was reached the details of the trip had been decided upon. As soon as we were comfortably settled in our different hotels and dinner attended to, the gentlemen began to gather in the rotunda of the Palace Hotel, which was known as the rendezvous of the party while in the city. Mr. Purdy, the Pennsylvania tourist agent, had secured a guide, and at nine o'clock we left the hotel and started for a six-hour walk in a quarter that is entirely given up to the Chinese, known familiarly as "Chinatown." Our party numbered fourteen, counting the guide, and a jolly party it was.

Leaving the Palace Hotel we passed up Market street, then into Kearney and California streets, and finally into Dupont street. The last-named street is in what is termed the French quarter, where degraded women sat in open windows to attract willing, susceptible and unsuspecting visitors to their apartments. Above the doors each inmate had her name painted in large letters. For two or three blocks on each side of the street the houses are given over to these women. As we hurried through this quarter an elderly German of our party remarked, "Dis ish von hell of a town," to which we all agreed.

Chinatown, as you enter it, presents a semi-respectable appearance. Large stores, filled with Chinese goods, attract the eyes and the pocket-book. Some small trinkets were bought, but as we were out sight-seeing and not shopping we hurried on. Passing a cheap restaurant we looked within, but that was all. The odor of the place did not encourage further investigation. At one of the stores some cakes were offered for sale. The guide told us they were made from sprouted beans, a basket of which was standing on the sidewalk. Eggs imported from China, done up in black mud, were on the counters. Beetles as large as one's thumb were sold by the dozen. Dried horned toads were recommended as a cure for rheumatism, a couple of which were handed us by way of a bid for business.

Chinese children, with their little pigtails hanging down their backs, were running through every street, making the air resound with their merry shouts. Men were hurrying to and fro, some bound for the gambling-dens which appear on every side and seem well patronized, and others on various errands, giving the whole place a lively appearance. Very few women were seen, as most of those brought to this country are employed in questionable and immoral diversions, and their owners keep a strict watch over them for fear some one will entice them into new fields of degradation. Chinese women are in high demand here since the Exclusion act was passed.

Going into a court of one of the large lodging-houses, several bags and baskets were noticed hanging to the wall. They were receptacles for waste paper. If a piece of paper should drop in the court the first Chinaman passing would pick it up and put it into one of the receptacles. The bags are emptied every day by the different societies, each of which has its own collector.

The paper is then taken to one of the Joss-houses, where it is burned.

Peering into one of the lodging-rooms, from which came a nauseous odor, a strange sight greeted us. Rows of narrow bunks, hardly wide enough for one man to lie in comfortably, reached from floor to ceiling. As many as forty Chinamen occupied one room. The only ventilation when the door was closed was secured through four auger-holes, two inches in diameter, bored in the top of the door. At one place the guide pointed out what resembled a pigeon-roost nailed to the side of one of the buildings. It was the home of four Chinamen. The dimensions of the box were about as follows: height, four feet; breadth, eighteen inches; length, about ten feet. It was reached by a ladder, and the last one up pulled the ladder in with him.

The Joss-house was next visited, and it was inspected with much curiosity by our company. A peculiarity of the Joss houses is that they always face the east. One of the several that we visited was located on the east side of the street, facing west (originally used for business or other purpose). To enter it we passed under an archway to what was formerly the rear of the building.

Here we saw a decidedly ornamental front, with a balcony extending the entire width of the building. At each end of the balcony sat an immense dragon, open-mouthed, and holding between its jaws a large ball. According to the belief of the Chinese the ball prevents the closing of the dragon's mouth and thus prevents the devil from bothering any of the members of the fraternity who contribute to the support of this particular Joss-house.

Entering, we climbed the stairs, noticing on the wall strips of paper covered with Chinese characters. They represented the amounts given by devotees for the support of the house. Going into the room the guide picked up some candles and incense-sticks, and explained the mode of worship and the offices of the different gods. The carvings in the temple were wonderful specimens of workmanship. Before leaving we were solicited to buy some incense-sticks to "bling gooda luck." Considerable time could have been spent examining the bronzes, armors and different paraphernalia of the house.

The theatre was the greatest treat. We went in through the actors' entrance, wound around upstairs and down, under pavements, through cellars and into all sorts of places, including the kitchen and sleeping-apartments of the employés, and finally landed in the dressing-room, where several of the actors were making their "toilet," and from there to the stage. The orchestra was on the back of the stage, in full view of the audience, and comprised several screeching stringed instruments, some tom-toms and a pair of immense cymbals that were continually clanging. Such music would drive a nervous person wild. The make up of the principal actor was indescribable. His head-rigging consisted of an immense crown of feathers and paper, with two feathers fully five feet long which he would grab occasionally and strut about the stage, much to our amusement. The audience was not an enthusiastic one, as the Chinese never applaud ; but woe to the actor who makes the least break in his part—he will be hissed off the stage. The men and women occupy different sections, the former having the first floor and the latter the gallery.

The Chinese never finish a play in one evening. It will sometimes run for six months before the entire play has been produced. The one we attended had been on the boards for three weeks, and three weeks longer would be required before the final act would be played.

Leaving the theatre we next visited an opium-joint. As the establishment was in the base-ment, we descended a rickety flight of steps leading to it. The fumes of the opium, as they were wafted up through the opening, were any-thing but pleasant, but as we were out sight see-ing we did not mind a little thing like that, and kept right on. The guide led the way, and making a misstep shot headlong into the middle of the room, much to the surprise of the keeper of the joint, who was not accustomed to see his patrons enter in such an undignified and hasty manner. As we entered, the villainous-looking proprietor, who sat in a small box-like compart-ment weighing out the drug, gave us a very severe scowl, but that did not deter us. The establishment was very poorly patronized on this occasion, as only two unfortunates were upon the hard shelves "hitting the pipe." The furnish-ing of the place was most primitive. On each side of the room was a shelf about seven or eight feet wide, upon which the patrons roasted their opium and inhaled the fumes of the noxious drug. It was upon this platform that the two men lay. When asked how they liked to smoke, the reply was, "Maka feela gooda." As we were leaving, other customers came down the steps, bought their supply of opium and started for the hard shelves, where they would soon be under the influence of the drug.

This was but one of the numerous opium-joints to be found in underground Chinatown, where the lazy and dissolute smokers and eaters of the drug spend their time and waste their energy. A Chinese scholar thus sums up the bad effects of opium, which, he says, is taken at first to raise the animal spirits and prevent lassitude : " It exhausts the animal spirits, impedes the regular performance of business, wastes the flesh and blood, dissipates every kind of property, renders the person ill-favored, promotes obscenity, violates the laws, attacks the vitals, and destroys life. In comparison with arsenic, I pronounce it tenfold the greater poison ; one swallows arsenic because he has lost his reputation, and is so involved that he cannot extricate himself. Thus driven to desperation, he takes the dose and is destroyed at once ; but those who smoke the drug are injured in many ways It may be compared to raising the wick of a lamp, which, while it increases the blaze, hastens the exhaustion of the oil and the extinction of the light. Hence, the youth who smoke will shorten their own days and cut off all hopes of posterity, leaving their parents and wives without any one on whom to depend. From the robust who smoke the flesh is gradually consumed and worn away, and the skin hangs like a bag. Their faces become cadaverous and black, and their bones naked as billets of wood. The habitual smokers doze for days over their pipes, without appetite ; when the desire for opium comes on, they cannot resist its impulse. Mucus flows from their nostrils and tears from their eyes ; their very bodies are rotten and putrid "

On our way to the restaurant, which was the next place visited, we stopped for a few moments in front of a Chinese barber-shop. Instead of the usual striped pole seen in front of our own shops, the sign displayed was very much like an old-fashioned umbrella-rack, made of four up rights, about three feet in height, and joined together. The victim was seated in a chair, in an upright position, and held a small tin plate, upon which the hair that was scraped off his head was placed. No lather was used, only water. Each customer, as he took his place in the chair, was presented with a pipe which would hold a very small portion of tobacco, suf- ficient for about two strong whiffs, when it would have to be replenished. A peculiar thing noticed was that the hairs within the ear were carefully cut out, the razor used for this purpose being very small and delicate.

Entering the building occupied by the restaurant, we found there were three grades of prices. On the first floor the cheapest fare was served, and the absence of furniture was noticeable. On the second the prices advanced and some attempt at furnishing was made, but on the third floor the prices were the highest and the furnishings were elaborate. We sat on stools of solid ebony, inlaid with mother of-pearl, and gazed upon tapestries worked with gold thread. Bronzes of fine workmanship were seen in different parts of the room. We all ordered tea at twenty five cents per cup Before our order was served a great quantity of sweetmeats were brought out and placed upon the table. Corn-cakes, almonds, preserved watermelon, plums, and a variety of Chinese dainties finished the feast. They were equal to any of the high-priced delicacies of our Eastern confectioners, and were given free with a cup of tea. The tea was served in small bouillon-cups, and poured from them into the cups for drinking. A pot of hot water was placed upon the table for use in case any one wanted to weaken his beverage.

This was the last place visited on the China-town trip, and as the hours had commenced to lengthen we sought our hotels, where we spent some time in the bath before retiring.

Our stay in San Francisco was necessarily short, as we had determined to visit the southernmost points of the trip before hot weather should come on and render traveling uncomfortable.

After bidding good-bye to those who had concluded to remain somewhat longer in San Francisco, nineteen of our party met in the ferry-house one morning to continue the trip. We were soon on the ferry-boat and out in the bay. All along the bay-front were immense wharves, alongside of which were vessels of all nations receiving and unloading freight. In due time we arrived at the Oakland wharf, where we disembarked, got into our sleeping-cars, and commenced our journey southward.

We were soon out of Oakland, but for a time were kept busy fighting flies which had taken possession of our car, and had determined on a personal inspection of every one who entered. After a successful skirmish, however, the enemy was routed, and we settled back in our cushioned seats to enjoy the scenery of the San Joaquin

Valley, which is known as the finest wheat
district in the world.   On either side of the road
were wheat-fields and vineyards (or groves) of
oranges, lemons, olives, apricots and figs.   Wild
flowers grow in abundance and are surpassingly
beautiful.   Neat towns, with pretty Spanish
names, are passed frequently.   In front of houses
were hedges of calla-lilies and geraniums.   It
was no uncommon thing to see geraniums reaching to the second story of the houses.   The
blossoms were of all colors—red, pink, white and
variegated.   Roses of all hues would climb as
high as the houses.   Occasionally we would
see a tree covered with roses, the bush having
spread over the entire tree.   Each succeeding
view appeared more beautiful than the last, and
it was a relief to our eyes when the curtain of
night was let down and shut out the delightful
panorama upon which we had looked all day.

On awaking in the morning we ascertained
that we had passed through the Mojave desert
and would soon be in Los Angeles, where we
were to change cars and proceed farther south.

Pulling out of Los Angeles we were rapidly
approaching our goal.   The lands we passed
through were not so well kept as those farther

north, excepting where the ranches and groves were irrigated.

Frequently we would pass over long trestles, built across sandy wastes, which we ascertained were the beds of rivers. In the winter and spring they are occupied by raging torrents, but now the snow had melted off the mountains and there remained nothing of the river but its sandy bed.

The farther south we go the more frequently appear the adobe houses. At Capistrano the train passed near the ruins of one of the old Spanish missions. It is in a fair state of preservation, services being still held in the chapel. It was built by the Franciscan Fathers, and was the finest church and mission constructed by that order in California. Its composition is adobe bricks and it is covered with red tile. The combined action of rain and an occasional earthquake has thrown down some of the walls, but the chapel still stands. An olive-orchard planted by the Monks can be seen from the car window. The trees are over one hundred years old and still bear bountifully. The Fathers have left, and the fields and orchards that once belonged to the mission are owned by other people.

Passing Capistrano the train soon came in sight of the ocean and then ran along the beach for several miles. The waves washed almost up to the road-bed, and the fresh sea-breeze from the ocean gave additional pleasure to the trip, as the day had been very warm and the cars like ovens.

The train soon passed through Old Town, as the original sight of San Diego is now known, and pulled into the handsome station at San Diego proper. Here we left the cars and took the 'bus for Coronado. It was but a short ride to the ferry that crosses San Diego Bay, the finest harbor south of San Francisco. It is entirely land locked, and vessels of the heaviest draught can anchor within it. Landing at Coronado we drove through a beautiful avenue, lined on either side with broad-leaved palms and stately eucalyptus trees, giving a most beautiful effect. As we approached the hotel the well-kept lawns and flower-beds attracted our attention. Especially interesting was a bed containing a great variety of cacti. There were probably forty varieties, from the symmetrical globe like plant to the gnarled and twisted member of the family which tried to send out branches in every direction.

The hotel is an immense building—not high, but covering a great deal of ground. It is built around an open court, where flowers of many varieties are growing. Tropical trees are abundant. Several fountains are continually playing, throwing their beautiful sprays into the warm sunlight and giving a cool and pleasant temperature to the atmosphere. Several pairs of the plumed California quail are kept within the court, and may be seen at all times darting here and there through the flowers and shrubbery. An enclosed veranda faces the ocean, where, during stormy weather, guests may sit and watch the raging ocean which belies its name. The views from the veranda are beautiful. Out in the ocean are the Coronado islands. Dead Man's Island, so named from its resemblance to a man laid in his grave-clothes, is pointed out to every visitor.

Point Lomo, the entrance to San Diego Bay, where the government has erected the highest light-house in the world, is plainly seen. In the evening we greatly enjoyed watching the alternate flashes of the red and white light.

The hotel is under the management of Mr. E. S. Babcock, a former resident of my native town, located in that portion of Illinois known as "Egypt." While living there he was a clerk in one of the principal business houses of the town, and was a general favorite among all classes with whom he came in contact.

Coronado Beach was our headquarters while we made excursions into the surrounding country. Our trips usually occupied about a day, so that we would only be away from the hotel during the mid-day meal, and that, in lunch form, the obliging proprietor always had in readiness for us when we left the hotel.

On the morning of the anniversary of the defeat and dethroning of Maximilian, a party of us made an excursion to Tia Juana, a Mexican town just across the border, expecting to see some of the national games played by the Mexicans. It was a delightful ride along the narrow strip of land which divided the ocean from the bay, and the cool winds, as they were wafted from either side, recompensed for the glare of the white sands of the beach. At National City we changed to a narrow-gauge road, and we were soon speeding toward our destination. The railroad passes through groves of lemon, orange and olive trees. On either side are many beautiful residences, embowered in forests of flowers. The air was laden with the perfume of the

blossoms of the orange and lemon trees, and
the fragrance of the flowers could not be equaled.
California is the home of flowers, and they grow
in profusion wherever the ground is irrigated.
At almost every station great quantities of
oranges and lemons were taken on the train to
be carried to the markets of San Diego, from
whence they were to be shipped either to San
Francisco or to the Eastern markets.   At one
of the stations, standing quite near the railroad,
was a large building known as the watch-factory.
The projectors of this enterprise made only a few
watches and then closed down.   The conductor
informed us that the time-pieces cost on an
average about $2,500 each, when the cost of
the business venture was fully estimated   The
building, like many others in this part of Lower
California, was decorated with the usual sign,
" For Sale."

After a ride of about two hours the train came
to a stop alongside of a weather-beaten building,
and the conductor called, " All out for Tia
Juana."   We alighted and followed the crowd
across a brook which went by the name of the
Tia Juana river.   The passage was made on a
foot-bridge, which consisted of a single plank,
and several of the party came near toppling over

into the water. Not twenty feet from the bridge
were several youngsters clad only in Nature's
garb, enjoying a mid-day bath. Like the aver·
age "Young America" these typical little Mexicans seemed not the least abashed, but viewed
our procession with an air of characteristic inno·
cence and curiosity. Thus one gets a touch
of Nature everywhere — provokingly obtrusive
though it sometimes is. A little distance from
the end of the bridge stood a couple of hacks to
convey us to the village and return upon the
payment of fifty cents each. One of the drivers,
an obliging negro, shouted at the top of his
voice that no one in the town could speak a
word of English, and that he would act as inter-
preter *gratis* to all of his passengers. This was
a business proposition of which we took advantage. It was a short trip over a dusty road to
the village. On reaching it we were somewhat
surprised to see many of the party who had
walked from the station ready to return. There
are not over a dozen buildings in the place, the
principal one being occupied as the custom-
house and post office. It is rectangular, and
built around an open court in which also were
the stables The building is only one story in

height, built of adobe, roofed with red tiles, and, like the others, was whitewashed.

It being a national holiday the post-office was closed, and many of the party were disappointed at not being able to send letters home from Mexico. Like all the residents of southern climes the post-master would not work on a holiday for anybody, and, although we offered him double price for postage stamps and cards, he would not open the office and sell them to us. In the room occupied by the collector of customs was one of the officers busily engaged in stamping the national emblem of Mexico on cards and handkerchiefs that the tourists had with them. The only places to visit were the stores, and the proprietors did a flourishing business in crude pottery and rag figures made by the Indians. As the time for departure drew near our loquacious guide made his appearance from one of the buildings where "meschal," the national beverage of the Mexicans, was sold. That he had in the *interim* been sampling the seductive fluid was evident. He had a number of bright Mexican dollars in his hands which he solicited us to purchase at the rate of one dollar and a half each. He did not appear at all abashed when we told him that we could buy them by the bushel in New York at the rate of sixty-five cents on the dollar.

On our return to the station we met several persons selling the great Mexican dish, "frijoles." It was done up in corn-husks, and had the appearance of hashed meat with a plentiful supply of thick catsup. A look was sufficient—a taste would have been fatal, we thought. As we crossed the bridge the U. S. custom officer was there ready to seize any cigars or "meschal" that the tourists had purchased in the village.

Before returning to San Diego we visited the great Sweetwater dam. It is a solid wall of masonry, ninety feet in height, and extends from one mountain to the other, across a narrow valley. It confines the winter flow of the Sweetwater river, and forms a reservoir of over seven hundred acres, holding enough water to supply a city of 50,000 inhabitants. It is from this reservoir that the water is supplied for the irrigating of the fruit ranches in the neighborhood of San Diego.

Passing through National City we had a good chance to see the evil effects of a "boom town." All along the road between this city and San Diego were houses in every stage of non-completion, which had been abandoned and left to the

mercy of the elements. Rows of business houses,
completed with the exception of the roof, were
frequently seen. A few years ago, when southern
California was booming, there were over twenty
thousand people on the ground of National City.
Now there are not over two thousand, and most
of them would like to get away.

Arriving at the hotel we found the corridors
filled with a party of Raymond tourists, number-
ing over three hundred. Among them we met
some very pleasant people, and the acquaintance
was kept up with many of them until our stay in
the West was completed. It was our good fortune here to meet a relative of our family who
was spending the winter at San Diego, and we
arranged for a trip the next day up the San Diego
valley to the old mission.

The morning dawned bright and clear, as all
mornings are in this balmy climate of southern
California. After a hearty breakfast we boarded
the cars which run from the hotel to the ferry,
and were soon across the bay and at the wharf at
San Diego, where our cousin, Mr. Lathan W.
Jones, was waiting with a span of spirited horses
to take us over to Oldtown and up the beautiful
San Diego valley to the old mission, after which
the valley was named.

San Diego is beautifully situated on the side of
a gently sloping hill which faces the San Diego
bay, the finest deep-water harbor south of San
Francisco.   Our course led us through the business portion of the new town, or what is now
called San Diego.   The old settlement is some
four miles back from the city of to-day.   The
streets were macadamized or laid with sheet asphaltum.   Cable and horse cars were going in
every direction, but business seemed dead.   The
town was trying to recuperate from the effects of ·
a "busted boom."   In 1887, when the "boom"
was at its height, over 60,000 people were on the
grounds, and land brought fabulous prices.   The
country for miles in every direction was staked
out for building lots, which were readily purchased by the excited arrivals from the Eastern
States.   To-day there are not over 15,000 people
who might be called residents of the place.
When the collapse came everything seemed to
fall to pieces.   A magnificent building, once the
quarters of a bank, is now used for the storage of
baled hay.   The vice-president of the concern
had just finished a handsome brown-stone residence, built with funds of the bank, when the
crash came.   He is now in Italy, where extra-
dition papers cannot be served on him to bring

him back to this country. Public buildings and school-houses were built on a grand scale, and bonds floated in the East for the payment of them. How these bonds will be met when they come due is a problem that must be solved some time in the future.

The road led us around the brow of the hill and along the grade of an abandoned motor railroad which had been built during the " boom," and connected the city with a small hamlet on False bay. The road never paid running expenses, and the rails were taken out and sold for old iron. We passed a number of very pretentious dwellings which had never been occupied and were rapidly going to decay. In several instances the roofs had fallen in and the walls were considerably out of plumb.

Reaching Oldtown, which was the place selected by Father Junipero Serra in 1769 for the first Roman Catholic mission in what is now California, we were attracted by the old adobe building which was once the fort, or presidio. It, like most houses built in warm climates, is rectangular in form and opens on a court within. The cells once occupied by the padres are rapidly going to decay, and are now used as stables. Some of the walls are about two feet in thick-

ness. One or two of the rooms not as yet appropriated for stabling purposes were covered with a
cheap wall-paper, evidently bought from some
of the trading vessels that used to coast along
these shores. After a good deal of hammering
and pulling, an old thumb latch from one of the
doors was secured to carry away as a memento of
the place. The building is only one story in
height and covered with red tiling. In front of
the entrance is a row of pepper trees, affording a
delightful shade, and under which the old missionaries no doubt spent many pleasant hours.
It was in this building that Helen Hunt Jackson's "Ramona" is said to have been married.

Not far from the presidio is the little Catholic
chapel, in which are quite a number of antique
paintings and statuary. In the rear, hard by,
are two old bells taken from the ruins of the old
mission. They are hanging on a rough scaffold,
which corresponds with the surroundings very
well. They were brought from Spain over a
century ago, and have Latin inscriptions on
them. Their tone is sweet and low, and must
have pealed forth merrily when the marriage of
"Ramona" was celebrated. Adjoining the
chapel is the old burial-ground, surrounded by
an adobe wall about four feet in height, which

is covered with a roof made of red tile. There was a deserted look about the place, and many of the graves were overgrown with weeds.

Near the presidio is the old Kanaka Hotel, which was the principal hostelry when San Diego was the centre of the hide trade for this part of the country. With the acquisition of California by the United States, the discovery of gold and the increased population, men drawn hither in search of wealth who thought that the Mexicans and Spaniards had no rights which Americans were bound to respect, and looked upon the herds of cattle belonging to the mis-sions as theirs by right of conquest, killed many of the cattle and appropriated them to their own use. The mission never recovered from this in road upon its resources, and from that time com-menced to decline. The old tannery is still there, but its business has sadly depreciated.

Not far from the neglected presidio are the ruins of the first mission. Very little remains of them, even of the foundation. The site is guarded by two large date palm trees protected by a neat whitewashed picket fence. These trees were said to have been planted soon after the mission was established, and are, consequently, over one hundred years old. An old Mexican

was working in the field near by and was asked
the course we should take to find the mission.
After giving us the information we desired, he
cautioned us to be particular as to where we
crossed the river, as there was a likelihood of
being caught in the quicksands which abound in
the rivers of this country.

The balmy air and the perfume from the many
flowers which grew in profusion on all sides
made the ride a most delightful one. The beautiful saffron and the brilliant red blossoms of the
cactus were seen on all sides. Orange, fig and
apricot orchards were growing wherever the owners could secure water for irrigation.

Noticing a gentleman approaching from the
direction of our course, and thinking that he was
a resident of the vicinity, from the fact that he
was carrying his coat on his arm and was proceeding along in a leisurely manner, we drew the
reins on our horses and stopped to inquire the
way. To our surprise we found him to be one of
our party who had started to walk to the mission, but was unable to cross the river and had
turned back. We invited him to a seat in our
carriage.

Some distance ahead of us was a carriage
going in the same direction as ourselves, so we

gave rein to our horses and were soon up to
them. Remembering the caution of the Mexican we let them lead the way, so that in case of
accident we would profit by their misfortune.
We had not gone very far when their driver
pulled to one side and got out and made some
motions as though repairing a break in the har-
ness, and let us pass. We were only a few rods
ahead of them when he jumped into the carriage
and drove after us. The ruse was successful.
He wanted us to lead and find the quicksands so
that *he could profit by our example*.

We forded the river without accident, proceeded up the road, and turning into a lane drove
up to the old mission. This was the second site
chosen by Father Junipero Serra, on account of
an uprising of the Indians, who destroyed the
first building at Oldtown. It is built on the
crown of a hill overlooking the valley of the San
Diego river. This commanding site was chosen
to guard against future surprises from the Indians, who were liable to rise up without warning
and take the good missionaries and torture them
in the most approved style of the Inquisition,
even going so far as to crucify a couple of them.
At one time there was a high wall surrounding
the entire mission, but the ravages of time and

weather have played havoc with it, and now only a small portion of it is standing. The chapel was used until quite recently, but late earthquakes have thrown down most of the walls. It has been the custom for some time for the sojourners at San Diego and Coronado to come out on excursions and use the chapel for a dancing-pavilion.

Recently some sisters of the Roman Catholic Church, through the co-operation of Miss Drexel, secured sufficient money to construct a frame building and established a school for Indian children, to teach them some of the arts of civilization and instill in their minds the elements of the Roman Catholic faith. We were shown through the entire building, from the kitchen to the dormitories, and noticed the particular pains taken to keep things neat and clean. It was recess, and most of the children were out in the yard playing. There were a number of half-breeds among them, and one or two in particular had unmistakable traces of African blood in their veins. The pure-blooded Indians had straight, raven-black hair, while those mixed with Caucasian blood had hair wavy and of a lighter shade. Those with African blood coursing in their veins were easily distinguished by the unmistakable sign—kinky hair.

At the base of the hill and along the river is a large olive orchard planted by the missionaries, and although over one hundred years old it still yields abundantly. The presses used by the padres for making the oil are there yet, but are idle, as there is an olive-oil factory in San Diego, where all the latest machinery is used, and the expense and labor required does not permit of the old methods.

We spent over an hour wandering around the place, and were loth to leave, as the associations were of peculiar interest and kept us putting off the moment of departure as long as possible.

Returning, our course led us down the valley and up a steep road to University Heights, where a pavilion had been erected and the grounds surrounding it laid out in flowers. In the basin of a fountain some of us saw for the first time the pink and purple water-lily. They are much larger than the white lily, and fully five inches in diameter. While waiting in the restaurant connected with the place several of our friends came in and a pleasant time was spent on the piazzas which overlooked the valley on one side and the city of San Diego on the other. This part of the city was laid out for the principal resident portion, and many pretentious dwellings were erected. Some are vacant, and almost every one is for sale.

When returning to the carriage we killed an immense tarantula which was seen moving along on the ground between the wheels of the carriage and over which the ladies had stepped on entering the conveyance. They afterwards declared that it caused a shudder every time they thought of how close they had been to the uncanny thing.

As we were driving back, our attention was directed to a gentleman who had come here with the expectation of building a fine residence and making it his permanent home. He bought several lots, deposited the balance of his cash (some $30,000) in the bank, and started to build. He first completed his stable, and was getting ready to start the dwelling when the crash came, and the bank in which his money was deposited went with the rest. Instead of completing his residence he finished up a few rooms in his stable and made that his home.

In time San Diego will recover from its setback, but it will be a long time. It will no doubt continue to be a resort for people in search of an equable climate, for no pleasanter nor more healthful place can be found in the country. The air seems to impart everything that the system requires For people having weak lungs a climate better adapted to their requirements cannot be found.

It was with many regrets that we repacked our valises and trunks preparatory to departure from our home-like quarters at the Coronado Hotel. The beautiful gardens that surround it on all sides will long be remembered, as well as the wonderful collection of cacti in the "Arizona" garden. Pleasant walks along the beach and on the hotel piazzas, where we drank in the health-giving ozone, will be looked back to with a great deal of pleasure. The evening hours passed in our rocking-chairs watching the alternate flashes of the red and white light of Point Lomo light-house, some eight miles to the north, at the entrance of San Diego Bay, will often be recalled when the mind is at rest from the cares of business, and the incidents of "Our Trip to California" are brought to memory.

At last the day came when we were to bid good-bye to some of our friends and commence to retrace our steps. Of the nineteen of our party who left San Francisco and came to San

Diego, only thirteen met in the waiting-room of
the neat railroad station of the latter place. Our
baggage having been looked after, we were soon
on the train with our faces to the north. Out of
San Diego and past Oldtown the train carried us
through a country rich in romance and story, but
prosy enough as one looked out of the car windows. Many small stations with pretty Spanish
names were passed. At each stop our attention
was drawn to the profusion of flowers that were
blooming in the yards along the railroad and at
the grounds surrounding the stations.

At Orange we changed cars to make a circuit-
ous trip through the district almost entirely devoted to orange culture. Irrigating canals were
seen in all directions, and the train passed
through numerous orange groves. The golden
fruit hanging in clusters, with a background of
dark green, made a beautiful picture. At almost
every station were large packing-houses where
the fruit was brought in, sorted, packed and
shipped to the markets.

Riverside is the centre of the orange market,
and is a city whose limits cover about twenty-
five thousand acres. The town proper has about
three thousand inhabitants. Most of the shade
trees are either orange or lemon. The principal

street is Magnolia avenue. It is the finest driveway in southern California. For more than eight miles both sides are shaded with eucalyptus, palm or magnolia trees, while the ranches on either side are devoted to lemon, orange, fig or grape culture. Our stay in Riverside was necessarily short, as we wished to reach Los Angeles early in the evening. Between the two cities are many thriving towns, as the buildings plainly show. The country is fertile, and only needs the water that is supplied by the irrigating ditches to make the greatest returns. The southern slope of all the mountains is devoted to raising grapes, from which the wine and raisins of California are produced.

It was after dusk when we arrived at Los Angeles, "The City of the Angels." Making Hotel Westminster our headquarters, we began planning our excursions to the surrounding resorts and places of interest.

Los Angeles, or to give it its full Spanish title, La Puebla de la Reina de les Angeles, literally the town of the Queen of the Angels, was settled in 1781. It is situated on the western slope of the coast range of southern California, and protected as it is from the chilling blasts of the Rocky Mountains, has a climate that invites one to tarry long within its bounds. The old adobe huts have disappeared before the brick and stone residences of modern times. The only thing to remind one of the ancient Spanish ownership is the old mission. It is located in that portion of the town which was formerly the central part, and faces an open plaza or park. The building is still in use and is in a fair state of preservation. The grounds surrounding it are enclosed by a high wall built of adobe. It is in the midst of a busy city, and stands as a memento of Spanish occupation.

The climate of the city being semi-tropical, most of the tropical plants are to be seen within the lawns which surround the palatial residences, and even in the front yards of the less imposing dwellings. If it was a fit place for the Queen of the Angels in 1781, it is certainly no less inviting now. It is a resort for people afflicted with lung troubles, and many, after staying here for several years, are to all appearances cured.

The city is well supplied with hotels and boarding-houses, and one can live remarkably cheap. If a person of limited means should go there it would be best to secure a room in a private family and procure meals at one of the many restaurants which can be found in the city. Most of the hotels are kept on the European plan, but our company uniformly chose the American plan when practicable. Hotel Westminster is the leading hotel of the latter class, and the proprietor, Mr. Johnson, is especially accommodating to all of his guests. It is centrally located, being not more than one square from any of the street-car lines which traverse the city in every direction. The writer has no hesitancy in recommending this hotel to any one who may peruse these pages.

The day following our arrival was Sunday, and was passed as a day of rest. We attended church in the morning, and the afternoon was consumed in writing letters to distant friends. In the evening, while out walking, we met some friends who had moved from the East and were living in the city. They had come to California for their health and were so well pleased with the climate that they had concluded to remain at Los Angeles and make it their permanent home.

Monday morning was spent in driving and visiting the several parks that belong to the city. The avenues are nearly all paved with sheet asphaltum, and are kept neat and clean. In the lawns and door-yards of the residences flowers

of every description bloom in luxuriance. In
several instances there were no fences on the
street-line, a hedge of calla-lilies answering the
purpose. Geraniums and other hardy plants
were frequently made to answer the purpose of
hedges. Eucalyptus and pepper are the principal
shade-trees. Some of the private grounds are
veritable fairy bowers, and seem to invite one
to remain within their bounds. Many of the
owners have signs inviting strangers to walk in
and enjoy what they can of the place. In order
to get an early start in the afternoon, we
returned to the hotel in time to get a lunch.
A carriage having been secured, we started for
an afternoon drive to Pasadena and through the
San Gabriel Valley.

Pasadena, although ten miles from Los Angeles, is connected with it by an avenue about
one hundred feet wide, and lined with groves of
orange and lemon trees   Many handsome villas,
with their well-kept lawns, are to be seen on
either side of the drive. Passing an orange
grove, our driver jumped over the fence and
brought an armload of the golden fruit to us.
The owners never object to any one helping
themselves, as there are frequently more oranges
than can be gathered. As we entered Pasadena

the orange groves gave way to magnificent lawns in which are growing almost every known tropical and semi-tropical plant. The central portion of the town is well equipped with handsome business houses, banks and an opera house. Passing through the city and out along avenues shaded with the stately eucalyptus trees, we climbed the hill to the Raymond Hotel, where the Raymond and Whitcomb tourists make their headquarters while in this section of California. It is situated on the top of a hill overlooking the entire San Gabriel Valley, and is approached by a winding road, both sides of which are lined with roses and flowers of every description. The season having ended, the hotel was closed when we arrived there, and after enjoying for a time the balmy air and beautiful view we drove on.

San Gabriel is a small settlement clustered around one of the old missions with which southern California was plentifully supplied. The village is distinctly Mexican in appearance and characteristics, and each person whom we asked for information shook his head and gave us to understand that he could not speak the English language. Driving up to the entrance of the mission the driver tried the door, but it was locked. He then went to the priest's resi-

dence, which adjoins the mission, and presently
the doors were swung open and there stood a
little, dried-up Spanish woman, who handed us
a small paper written in English, stating that
no one was to be admitted for less than twenty-
five cents. Whenever we would ask for information concerning the mission and the founding of
it she would shake her head and mutter
something in Spanish which we could not
understand. After looking at the old pictures
and statuary we took our places in the carriage,
when an old cripple came up and presented a
paper stating that he had a figure of the Virgin
and some sacred relics in his house, and inviting
us to come and see them. Dropping a piece
of silver in his hand he took off his hat, and,
making a very profound bow, repeated, "Mucha
gracio, señor," to which we replied "Adio,"
and drove off.

The entire village is constructed of adobe, and
presents a very picturesque scene. The mission
building is in a good state of preservation, and
services are held within its sacred walls. The
streets are narrow, and most of the houses are
built on the line of the street. The ruins of the
old presidio will soon be gone, as the ground
upon which they stand is too valuable to remain

unproductive. The belfry adjoining the mission
has a chime of four bells, and they peal out on
the evening air the curfew which calls the faith-

Bell Tower, San Gabriel Mission.

ful to offer up their evening prayers for the dying
day. The bells are hung in separate niches, and
the rope is attached to the clapper of each bell.

The mission was founded in 1804, and had almost fallen into decay when a few years since it was restored by putting in new arches to support a new roof. The pepper trees, which appear to have been the favorite shade with the padres, are found at the entrance of the building.

On our return to Los Angeles we visited the San Gabriel Winery and walked through the cellars in which are stored hundreds of thousands of gallons of wine. One cask alone holds fifty thousand gallons. We were all invited to taste the products of the grape, and all partook excepting the temperance contingent of the party. This valley, named after the patron saint of the mission, San Gabriel, is the best adapted to the wine grape culture of any in California, and the vineyards cover an immense area.

Returning to the hotel, we were somewhat surprised to meet a large party of the Raymond excursionists whom we had left in San Diego. They were on their way to the Yosemite Valley, and were stopping for the night in Los Angeles.

The following morning was devoted to shopping by the ladies of the party, while the gentlemen arranged their finances by getting drafts cashed and drawing upon their letters of credit.

It was a pleasant afternoon when our party, now reduced to eleven, took their seats in the car and were once more seeking new provinces to explore. We were soon rolling out of Los Angeles over a country which but a few years since was used for sheep herding, and in some places was a sandy waste, but which is now blooming with flowers and fragrant with orange blossoms.

We followed the main line of the railroad until a small station named Saugus was reached, where we branched off and entered the fertile valley of Santa Clara of the South. The railroad follows the river most of the way, excepting where the road makes a short cut across the valley and the river makes a long detour. On either side are the mountains, which rear themselves high into the clouds and form natural barriers to the cold winds from the Rockies, and also protect the valley from the storms from the Pacific ocean. The clouds lay like banks of snow against the mountains and seemed to temper the air and make it cool and balmy.

It was our fortune to meet a gentleman on the train who was acquainted with every point of interest along the road. To him we were very much indebted for the pleasant afternoon passed while riding along this beautiful valley.

He called our attention to many points of interest, which would have been passed unnoticed had it not been for him. Before we reached Camulos he pointed out the house described by Mrs. Helen Hunt Jackson as the home of "Ramona." The house is surrounded by a large orange grove, adjacent to which is a large olive orchard. The Santa Clara river flows through the ranch, and on its banks are clumps of willows and groves of wide spreading sycamores. It is no wonder that the scene of "Ramona" is laid in this beautiful valley, as it combines every element that could be desired for a book of the character of Mrs. Jackson's works.

Leaving the scenes of "Ramona," we soon enter a country which reminds one of the oil regions of Pennsylvania, but upon a much smaller scale. The principal oil-wells are some distance from the railroad, although most of the large tanks are located along the road, the oil being piped from the wells a few miles out in the mountains.

The whole valley of Santa Clara is rich and fertile, and will produce anything that grows in the way of fruits, grain and vegetables. We passed through one ranch where over two thousand acres were devoted to the raising of beans.

It would be a paradise to New Englanders who wish to escape the wintry blasts from the bleak shores of their native clime, as here they could revel in their favorite dish—baked beans. At several stations were large warehouses in which beans were stored like wheat in our own country.

At San Buenaventura, or, as the brakeman called it, "Ventura," the road leaves the valley and runs along the beach, and the green waters of the Pacific ocean roll up to the rock ballast of the road-bed. The pleasant ocean breeze was wafted through the cars, and, tempered by the balmy air from the valley, made us wish that we could stop and take up our abode in this part of California, where, according to reports, no one ever dies. When they wish to be translated they move to some Eastern State and there lie down and die.

It was about six o'clock when we reached the station at Santa Barbara. A short ride in the omnibus took us to the Arlington Hotel, where we were shown our rooms, and after changing our dusty linen for some fresh and clean we were ready for the dinner which was prepared for us. After partaking of the evening meal those of us who felt like it went out for a walk through the resident portion of the place.

Like all cities of southern California, tropical
plants of every description were growing in the
lawns and front yards of every dwelling. In
the lawn surrounding the hotel was a large rose-
bush reaching to the top of the four-story annex
of the hotel. There must have been a wagon-
load of roses on it. It covered a tree which grew
near the piazza, and gave it the appearance of
an immense mound of roses.

In the morning, after visiting most of the
novelty stores, including those kept by the Chinese, we took a street-car and rode to the old
mission at the foot-hills of the Santa Ynez Mountains, some two or three miles back from the
present city of Santa Barbara. After riding as
far as the cars went, we had to walk about a
mile before reaching the object of our visit.

The mission of Santa Barbara is without doubt
the best preserved of the many missions established along the coast of California, reaching
from San Francisco on the north to the Mexican
boundary on the south. The date of the founding of the mission is December 4th, 1786,
although Father Junipero Serra had established
a sort of military post on the same site some two
years previous. It was on the day of the cele-
bration of the feast of Santa Barbara that the

mission was founded and the cross raised. Like all the missions established in this part of the country, it received grants from Spain of all the best land in the vicinity, and by trading with the vessels that cruised along this coast in after years became very wealthy. Its greatest prosperity was reached in 1812, when the government of Spain, becoming impoverished by its excesses, commenced making demands upon the wealthy missions of this coast, and Santa Barbara was not missed. It then commenced to decline. The withdrawal of the protection of the military by the Mexican government hastened the downfall of this particular mission.

At the entrance to the plaza in front of the mission is the old fountain erected by the Franciscan Fathers during the palmy days of their existence. The front of the building once occupied by the Fathers is ornamented with a row of columns surmounted by arches which extend the whole length of the building. Back of the pillars is an open corridor with flag flooring. We mounted the steps and were soon within the cool shade, and seating ourselves upon the wooden benches that were placed along the wall we looked far out on the mild Pacific ocean, and then at the town of Santa Barbara at our feet.

We walked through the corridor to the entrance of the church, and, pushing open the ponderous oaken doors, entered. After walking up and down the aisles and looking at pictures, all of which were painted by Indians, we returned to the corridor. Going to one of the doors we pulled the bell, which was answered by an old monk dressed in hassock and cowl, who invited us into the reception-room, where we were requested to register our names. The monk refuted with some emphasis the implication that he was a Mexican. He said that there were none of them in the building. We were unable to go through the compartments and look into the cells, as the rest of the monks were at their devotions and could not be disturbed. After trying to get some information as to the surroundings and history of the place we returned to the city. We had intended going to see the mammoth grape-vine, but on account of a misunderstanding as to the time of starting, the visit was deferred.

The return to Los Angeles was without incident, excepting that we stopped for luncheon at one of the restaurants and bought some sandwiches which we were unable to eat. But this was not owing to poor appetites, as each member of our party can testify to. At Saugus our company was further decreased by three, who left the train and proceeded to San Francisco, while we returned to Los Angeles.

It was quite late in the evening when we arrived at Los Angeles, and upon reaching the hotel were somewhat surprised to meet three of our party whom we had left in San Francisco in the early part of the month. They had visited a number of the points of interest in and around the latter city, and were now commencing on the resorts in the southern part of the State. As they were to return East by one of the southern routes, it was necessary that they should visit the points of interest in the upper part of the State before coming south. Having several days to remain in the vicinity of Los Angeles we invited them to join our party, which they did. The evening was pleasantly spent in relating experiences which had happened since we had separated. Nearly every one had from one to three stories to relate, and the consequence was that it was very late before we retired.

Having decided to visit Redondo Beach the next morning, all were ready at an early hour to take the first train leaving Los Angeles for the beach. We were all at the station some time

before the train was ready to start, and the gate-
man very kindly allowed us to get into the cars
in order that we might escape the jam that always occurs at the gates.

The country through which we passed was a
succession of orange groves and orchards, and
occasionally a long strip of uncultivated country.
At many of the stations were the packing-houses
for oranges, and wherever we stopped the oranges
were free and we helped ourselves most industri-
ously.

Arriving at Redondo Beach we proceeded at
once to the hotel, the principal building in the
place. It is built upon the bluff and overlooks
the entire bay. It is a new house, and is furnished completely with all the modern con-
veniences. While we were waiting for our lunch
the manager showed us through the building and
took us into the ball-room, which was very pret-
tily decorated with flags and tropical plants.
The furniture of all the bed-rooms was new, and
had Redondo consisted of anything but a few
houses and the hotel we should have been
tempted to remain there a few days to breathe in
the health-giving air which came uncontaminated from the ocean. In front of the hotel, and
reaching to the plaza at the foot of the bluff,

were numerous beds of flowers of every variety, blooming in luxuriance. Back of the hotel was the menagerie, at this time containing only a playful bear. As there was some time to spare before luncheon was served, it was employed in walking along the beach and visiting the bathing grounds. The bath-houses have been erected so that they will not obstruct the view from the piazzas, which extend along the entire front of the hotel. The bay is a beautiful sheet of water, though at this time there was considerable sea-weed floating on its surface. The temperature of the water being quite low, none of us were tempted to take a "plunge."

After lunch, and before train-time, we amused ourselves hunting up souvenirs and watching the youngsters fishing on the pier adjoining the railroad station. One of the employés connected with the pier had captured a small seal and placed it in a tank on the pier. A windmill had been erected and was kept going constantly, pumping water from the bay into the tank. The seal had become quite tame and would come to the surface when called. He went by the name of "Jack," and was quite playful. The boys would bring him fish occasionally,

which he would devour with the greatest satis-
faction.

Returning to Los Angeles, which we reached
early in the afternoon, we ascertained that we
could easily make the trip to Santa Monica
before supper-time. We did not have to wait
very long before the train started, and we were
once more passing through orange groves, orchards and vineyards, and past pretty stations
which seemed almost embowered in flowers. It
was early in the evening when the train pulled
into the station at Santa Monica, and it was
only a short drive to the hotel, built upon a
bluff overlooking the beautiful bay of Santa
Monica. Our rooms were on the bay side, and
the constant splash and moan of the waves disturbed us somewhat, but before midnight we
had become used to it and enjoyed a pleasant
sleep. Like all hotels in this part of the country
the grounds surrounding it were tastefully laid
off in lawns and flower-beds, and at each meal
a fresh bouquet was placed on our table.

At breakfast it was decided to visit the ostrich
farm, some two or three miles from the hotel.
The most direct communication being by horse-
car, we all boarded one that passed the door.
The ride was a pleasant one, the open cars

enabling us to drink in the balmy air, tempered as it was with a slight breeze from the bay. Every breath seemed to give a new lease on life, and the ride was over before we could fully realize it.

Arriving at the farm, whic'i is enclosed with a high board-fence, the keeper met us at the gate and admitted us to the enclosure. Of course our attention was first given to the ostriches, of which there must have been at least three dozen inside the pens. They are ungainly birds, but very curious to observe and study. At our request the keeper gave them something to eat, which consisted of cabbage or cauliflower cut into small pieces. They would gather into their mouths a mass about as large as a man's fist and then swallow it. This big lump would move slowly down the long neck of the ostrich until it would disappear in the body. They were especially fond of bright things, and several of our party came near losing watch-charms and ear-rings, which the big birds would snap at. There is a store connected with the farm, where feathers, fans and eggs can be bought. Some of the party invested quite heavily in feathers and fans. In addition to the ostriches there is quite a menagerie connected with the place. There are a number of monkeys, badgers, bears, parrots, and one wildcat. The keeper informed us that there was at one time a great many more ostriches on the farm, but they had been scattered around at a number of resorts where they were placed on exhibition, as that paid a great deal better than the feathers alone. All eggs are hatched in an incubator at one of the ranches in the interior of the State, where the young birds are kept until they are able to withstand the damp winds that sometimes come from the ocean. After remaining some time — probably two hours — within the enclosure, we again boarded a street car and returned to the hotel.

Having plenty of time to spare before lunch, we went shopping and returned with our arms and hands full of souvenirs and curiosities. There being six ladies in the party, one can readily imagine how long it took to purchase these packages. On our return to the hotel we walked along the ocean-drive, a beautiful avenue which runs along the bluff overlooking the bay. On the side adjoining the cliff are magnificent groves of eucalyptus and other tropical trees, while scattered here and there are small pavilions and also a large stand where the band from the Soldiers' Home plays on certain evenings. On the opposite side of the avenue are the residences of the wealthy inhabitants of the town.

Noticing a great number of old men in veterans' clothes, we ascertained that the California Soldiers' Home was located about three miles from the city, and we concluded to visit it during the afternoon.

After dinner we secured a carriage and started for the Santa Monica cañon. It was a pleasant drive through avenues of eucalyptus trees and past fields ripe with waving grain waiting for the reapers to harvest. Going out past the Soldiers' Home and up a road which led through an immense wheat-field we soon reached one of the entrances to the cañon. Driving down the steep road into the valley we were soon in a romantic glen, with almost impenetrable thickets of flowers on either side of the narrow road. A little further up was an opening and the small cabin of a sheep-herder. There was no one at home, as the occupant had driven his flock further up the cañon, and it was too early to return for the night. We drove several miles further up the cañon, but found that we would not be able to reach the finest part of it and return in time to catch the last train for Los Angeles, so we turned about and started back. As we passed

along we gathered several large bouquets and
carried them to the station to take away with us.
Upon going to the hotel and settling our bills we
were presented by the proprietor's wife with a
large bouquet which she had plucked from an
immense rose-bush that grew at the edge of the
piazza.

We very much desired to remain longer at this
resort, but our time was getting short, and we
felt impelled to make our way to San Francisco
in order to secure passage with some friends who
had determined upon taking the trip to Alaska
before returning to the East. By the time the
train was made up we were in our places facing
towards Los Angeles.

CHAPTER III.

YOSEMITE VALLEY.

IT was Friday afternoon when we returned to Los Angeles for the last time. After a conference with the remaining members of our party it was decided to remain in the city until Monday afternoon, when we would start for the Yosemite Valley. Our party had now dwindled to eight, and it seemed probable that we should keep together. Saturday was spent in revisiting the pleasure-grounds and parks of the city and purchasing souvenirs. While engaged in the latter occupation we were most agreeably surprised to meet one of the chaperons of the Pennsylvania railroad who had made the trip overland with us. She was to remain in southern California much longer than we could, and in all likelihood would spend the entire summer on the Pacific coast Sunday was passed as a day of rest, and we enjoyed every minute of it. In the evening some friends came in and made us the last calls and gave us messages to carry to their friends in the East.

Monday was a busy day. The morning was

devoted to repacking our trunks and securing
tickets for sleeping car berths and seats in the
stages going into the Yosemite Valley. They
had all been ordered Friday evening, but it was
uncertain that we could secure Pullman accommodations on account of the great number of
delegates going to a Democratic State convention
to be held at Fresno, a station some distance up
the road.

Having bade good-bye to those of our party
who were to go further south, and a number of
friends who had called upon us, we were ready
to start. At two o'clock in the afternoon we
were all seated in the Pullman car waiting for
the train to pull out of the station. The train
was a very heavy one, there being twelve cars
attached to the engine. Six of them were sleeping-cars and the balance were either day-coaches
or heavily loaded baggage-cars. We moved
slowly out of the station, but were soon outside the city limits and going at a fair rate of
speed Looking out of the car windows we
bade farewell to Los Angeles, the "City of the
Angels," and wondered if it would be our pleasure once more to visit its blooming gardens and
pleasant drives, and to mingle with scenes and
associations that had become very dear to us.

We next entered the San Fernando Valley and passed through orange groves and olive orchards almost innumerable. Soon we noticed the train beginning to slacken its speed, and it was evident that we were ascending a grade. We climbed the San Fernando Mountains until we reached the tunnel, where as we entered we took the last look at the fertile fields and groves of the San Fernando Valley. The train, having passed the highest point, now began the descent, and our speed was perceptibly increased. At Saugus the cars, filled with passengers for Santa Barbara, were switched off and another Pullman sleeper loaded with Raymond excursionists was taken on. We followed the course of the Santa Clara river for quite a distance, until we entered the Soledad Pass.

Emerging from the Soledad Pass we entered the Mojave Desert. Having heard so much about the giant cactus or Yucca palm, which grows to a great height in this desert, the prospect on entering was more pleasing than when we crossed the desert from Ogden to the Humboldt Sinks in Nevada. These cacti grow to the size of trees, and with their club-like limbs, devoid of leaves, remind one of an immense forest recently swept with fire. An English

8

company started a plant to manufacture paper from the fibre of this palm. The experiment had not been a success financially, and the plant was abandoned. Another interesting feature was the buttes which rise from the desert on all sides. They are isolated hills, varying from two hundred to five hundred feet in height. Their sides are cut and grooved as if torrents of water had rushed down them. Unbidding as it seemed to us, there were yet several small villages and towns scattered along the line of the road. What they were there for, or what could induce any one to settle in this country, is hard to determine. The water which they use must be brought in pipes or ditches from the mountains, miles distant Some of the homes looked cheerful and inviting, but it will probably never be known why men settle in a country where it never rains and where the storms are sand-clouds. We passed Mojave and commenced the ascent of another range of mountains. As it was night, we were unable to see the loop of the Tehachapi Pass, where the road in making the descent of the mountains runs under its own tracks.

Most of the passengers in our car were delegates to the convention, and no sooner had the train left Los Angeles than they settled down for a good time. The porter brought in tables, and soon several games of poker were progressing finely. The stakes were not high, as they played what they told me was "a quarter limit." They had a plentiful supply of wine and beer in the smoking-room, and the porter was kept busy carrying cold beer and wine from the ice-chest to the players. Notwithstanding the lively absorption of liquors, none of the men became intoxicated.

In addition to the delegates there were two ladies going to Marysville, a city some distance north of San Francisco, on the road to Portland. One of them was the mother of two very interesting little children, who accompanied her. The children, a boy and a girl, took a great fancy to the writer, and persisted in destroying several beautiful bouquets in order that they might decorate him to their fancy. They wove wreaths for his hair, decorated his face with flowers, and in other ways amused themselves at his expense. They were especially bright children, and it was a pleasure to have them around. At first the mother was fearful that their actions might seem rude, but soon both she and her sister offered some suggestions as to the manner of placing the flowers in order to bring out the best effect. It was one of the most enjoyable afternoons spent while on the trip, and when the little tots retired for the night they expressed a reluctant good-bye and gave their willing subject a cordial invitation to stop off at their home and pay them a visit. We retired early, as we were expecting to be called at three o'clock in order to change cars at Berenda and proceed to the Yosemite Valley.

We were all soundly sleeping when, at midnight, the train came to a sudden standstill and almost threw us out of our berths. The delegates, however, slept soundly through it, as none of their heads were sticking out from the curtains of the berths wanting to know what had happened. When the porter came through the car we ascertained that the engine had broken down and it was a matter of conjecture as to when we would start. We were jerked about for a considerable time, but the engine was unable to pull the train, and a brakeman was sent back nine miles to the first station to telegraph for another engine. We tried to sleep, but the engine kept up a continual puffing and snorting until finally it was decided to send our disabled engine ahead with the baggage-cars and leave the pas-

sengers to be brought along by the extra, which
would arrive some time later. We then dozed off
and slept until the gray streaks of dawn had
made their appearance above the mountains.

Going out on the platform, it was ascertained
that we were in one of those valleys of southern
California where not a tree of any sort can be
seen except around the homes of the farmers
who have brought them from some nursery and
kept them alive by irrigation. Not far from the
railroad was a large irrigating ditch which supplied the adjacent ranches. The water was
brought from some reservoir up in the mountains, where the melting snow was stored and
then distributed by the canals to the ranches
along its course.

It was not long before the delegates began to
appear, and the time that elapsed before the arrival of the extra engine was pleasantly spent in
cracking jokes—several facetious individuals remarking that the presence of so many Democrats
was enough to "hoodoo" anything. When the
engine arrived we were eight hours behind time.
It was not long before we were flying up the
valley, and going at a rate of speed that showed
that the engineer was trying to make up for the
delay.

For the want of something more interesting
we employed our time in watching for ground-
squirrels and owls. They live together underground, and at almost every mound which sur-
rounds the openings to their habitations one or
two of these little open-faced birds were to be
seen. They had the appearance of being asleep,
and did not notice the train as we rushed by.
The squirrels were frequently seen sitting upon
their haunches on the tops of the little mounds,
but upon the approach of the train they would
disappear in an instant. They did not venture
far from cover while in search of their morning
meals on account of the numerous hawks which
were hovering around ready to swoop down upon
the little creatures and devour them.

It was about noon when we arrived at Berenda, where we changed cars and took a branch
road up to Raymond, where we were to take the
stages for a steady ride of a day and a half before
we would reach the head of the Yosemite Valley.

At Raymond we halted only long enough to
eat a fairly good dinner, when eight stages drove
up to the door and we took our places in the
seats assigned us before leaving Los Angeles.
Our stage was the last to drive up and was of
the old Concord pattern. Instead of springs

there were strips of leather bound together, reaching from the trunk-boot to the driver's box. which gave the body of the coach a rocking motion when the first shock of striking an obstruction was over. The writer, acting upon the suggestion of a friend, had secured a seat in the box with the driver, and we started off with high expectations. Our coach was in charge of Ed. Crawford, a veteran stage-driver, and it was a pleasure to see him handle the "ribbons" and guide the leaders around the sharp turns in the road. He was a little reserved at first, but upon being drawn out became quite talkative, and his fund of anecdotes made the ride very pleasant. The whip handle used by him was silver-mounted, and had been presented him by one of his admiring friends.

He called our attention to a number of trees which had the appearance of having been used for targets, as the bark was punctured with holes about the size of a bullet. He told us that the woodpeckers had drilled holes in the bark and filled them with acorns for winter's use. A pair of these birds would take possession of a tree, and after they had laid in their winter's supply of acorns would sit in the branches and guard

them with the greatest of care and fight viciously
to defend their possessions.

The first part of the ride was something new,
and we did not mind the jerks and jars to which
we were subjected, always hoping, however,
that the one just passed would be the last. The
road winds around the hills and mountains, and
frequently the gentlemen and many of the ladies
would get out to gather flowers and take a short
cut up the hill and reach a turn in the road long
before the stages would come up. It gave them
a chance to rest themselves from the sitting
position and also relieved the horses of considerable weight to drag up the hills. On all sides
in the open patches were flowers in great profusion, representing all colors of the rainbow,
but the most beautiful of all was the Mariposa
lily. It is a delicate flower, and the three leaves
strongly resemble the butterfly, from whence it
derives its name—"Mariposa" being the Spanish for butterfly.

When we started from Raymond the roads
were in fair condition, but after a couple of
hours we struck the mountain roads, which were
very rough, and on account of the recent rains
were full of chuck holes. Our driver exercised
as much care as possible, but those inside of the

coach received such a shaking up as they wish never to experience again.

In the middle of the afternoon we met a large party of Raymond excursionists. They were returning from the valley and were very enthusiastic over the scenery.

At every relay of horses the occupants of each stage would get down from their places and spread the blankets and robes on the ground and thus rest themselves for a few moments. There was a scarcity of cold water, and at several places refreshment stands were in operation. The signs displayed invariably told of "Ice-cold limonade," &c., but when one came to purchase, the drinks were warm and the price was "two bits," or twenty five cents each.

Each relay had its name, but the one most remarkable was "Grub Gulch." It was an abandoned mining camp, and at this time there were only a few shanties and a large building which served as hotel, store, saloon and post-office. The hills and valleys were covered with holes dug by prospectors in search of gold. There was an abandoned quartz-mill near the shaft of a mine also abandoned. The small amount of gold secured did not pay for the labor, and these holes and the old mill are all that now

show that gold was once sought for in this
region.

It was supper-time when we arrived at Grant's
—the dinner-station. There was a well cooked
meal awaiting us, which we ate with as much
haste as was conducive to good digestion in
order that we might get as far on the road as
possible before nightfall, as we had six full
hours to ride before reaching Wawona, the
supper-station, where we would remain over
night.

By the time we were ready to start we had
become very well acquainted with many of the
party, which added much to the enjoyment of
the trip. The roads were getting rougher, and
it was almost impossible to keep one's seat.
When we had a steep road we were glad to get
out and walk until the summit was reached, in
order to rest and take in some of the magnificent
views that were to be seen at every turn.

We had not proceeded very far when the
shades of night began to close around us, and
the reflectors at the head of the stages were all
lighted. They were of little use, however, as
they had not been cleaned for so long that the
intelligent horses on the lead could get along as
well without them. It was after nine o'clock,

when everything was quiet and some of us were trying to do a little dozing between jolts, that we were roused from our lethargy by a series of ear-splitting yells which resounded over the mountains and valleys. These were answered by others of similar character far up the mountain. We all wanted to know what it meant, and imagined all sorts of horrible things about stage-robbers and wild Indians. Crawford merely laughed and told us that the driver of the leading stage was calling to the men at the relay to have the horses ready when we arrived.

While we were waiting for the change to be made, our stage being the last to arrive and consequently the last to be attended to, we employed the time in examining one of the large trees which grew near the stable. It was at least ten feet in diameter, and there was not a branch to mar its symmetry for over one hundred feet from the ground We were all glad to hear Crawford call "All aboard," and soon were occupying our places. Cracking his whip, the four horses started off at a lively rate, and soon we were lost in the gloom of the forest. The stage-drivers kept up a constant calling to each other in order not to get too far separated, so that in case of accident aid would be near at hand.

The roads seemed to get worse, and at every opportunity we would get out and walk. Climbing those hills was tiresome, but it was much more pleasant to walk than to ride.

It was half-past one o'clock in the morning when our stage drove up to Major Washburn's hotel at Wawona, and we got out and registered our names. It was fully half an hour before we were shown to our rooms. Three hours of disturbed rest followed, when we were called in order to get an early start and reach the head of the Yosemite Valley by noon.

When our party assembled we found one who was unable to continue the trip. The shaking-up she had received and the tiresome night-ride had so exhausted her already delicate constitution that it would have been dangerous to have taken her further into the valley. Major Washburn's family very kindly offered to take the best care of her and try to have her in a condition to go out of the valley upon our return. We bade her good-bye and started off. Before proceeding many miles we all wished ourselves back at Wawona, and even out of the valley. The road became nothing but a series of chuck-holes, and the continued jolting we received kept all busy trying to keep on the seats. Our driver, between jolts, gave us a history of the discovery of the Yosemite. In the spring of 1851, Captain Boling, with a company of soldiers, while in pursuit of a band of marauding Indians who had retreated into these mountain fastnesses (considering it inaccessible to the whites), was the first white man to behold its sublimity and grandeur. The company had many narrow escapes from the savages, but finally, after subduing them, returned to civilization. It was the unanimous opinion of our party, after the rough ride of the past two days, that it was a pity the whole company had not been shot and scalped before they could have returned and reported their discovery to a gullible public. We changed our minds, however, before we left the valley.

The scenery was grand. At every turn of the road a new and wonderful view greeted our vision. Rounding some points the views that would burst upon us were beyond the power of description. In the foreground would be the tall and stately sugar-pine trees, from one to three feet in diameter, whose symmetrical trunks would tower from one hundred to one hundred and fifty feet above us before a single shoot or branch would appear ; then down into the valley and on the other side were the tall peaks, with their rugged sides, and in some cases their summits covered with snow. The air was so clear and the distance so deceiving that the driver asked us how far we supposed those mountains were from us ; the most of us guessed three or four miles, but he only laughed and said, "Well, I would not want to walk it for less than eight miles "

The roads in some places were in a fearful condition, and at one turn we all had to get out and walk up the mountain a short distance to relieve the horses, so that they could pull through a stretch of sticky clay, which had about the same tenacity as the blue and black mud of southern Illinois. Why roads should be allowed to remain in that condition in a country where stones are so plentiful as here cannot be understood, unless it is that the proprietors of the turnpike do not want to spend any money upon it, knowing that if people wish to come into the valley this is the shortest way.

Our first view of the Yosemite Valley proper was obtained when we rounded Inspiration Point. Here the stages all stopped and gave us an opportunity to get out and have a good look up and down the valley. The fifteen min-utes which we stood there, feasting our wonder-ing eyes upon the valley, and the peaks and domes that surround it, were too short, and it was with some reluctance that we returned to the stages and drove on. El Capitan, standing out like an immense fortress, was the first to greet our wondering eyes. It stands there with almost perpendicular sides, 3,300 feet above the level of the valley. It is granite, and does not have that dirty, rusty appearance of the other mountains over which we had just passed. Turning a little to the right we beheld a beautiful waterfall, which many of us took to be the Yosemite, but the driver soon corrected our mistake by telling us that it was the Bridal Veil Falls, and that we would not see the Yosemite Falls until we reached the floor of the valley and had pro-ceeded quite a distance toward the head of it.

The horses having been given a breathing spell, we were called to our seats in the stage, when the driver cracked his whip and off the four horses started on a gallop. The road from Inspiration Point to the floor of the valley is zigzag, and frequently the stages that had started ahead of us were seen on the ledge below,

apparently going in the opposite direction from
that which our horses' heads indicated. In some
places only a foot or two of rock intervened between us and certain destruction. Had the
driver been less steady in guiding his leaders
we should have been thrown over the precipice
into the valley thousands of feet below. The
least miscalculation would have been quite an
item to the life insurance companies that had
risks on several members of our party. As it
was, a few of them became somewhat nervous as
the four horses would gallop around some of the
sharp turns in the road without the least diminu-
tion of speed. They would all unconsciously
hug the side of the stage farthest from the edge
of the precipice and give a sigh of relief when
the straight road was reached.

Arriving at the level of the valley the road led
us quite near the Bridal Veil Falls, and the
driver drew rein to give us a chance to watch
the water as it came plunging over the precipice
some six hundred feet above. The mist arose in
great clouds and was wafted first in one direction
and then in another by the wind that continually
blows at the foot of the falls. On the opposite
side of the valley is another falls with the
name of the Maiden's Tears. She is said to be

weeping on account of not being able to get the bridal veil.

The Three Brothers.

Near the Bridal Veil Falls are a series of peaks sometimes called the Three Graces, but more

9

frequently the Three Sisters (companions of the
Three Brothers, which stand on the opposite
side of the valley). Near the former are the
Cathedral Rocks, which stand out prominently
against the sky, and as we passed on the Cathedral Spires came into view. They are two
majestic columns which rise in close proximity
to each other, several hundred feet above the
mountain upon which they stand, and the name
given them is not at all inappropriate. One of
the spires has a large piece broken off, giving
it an odd appearance. The piece detached was
thrown down several years ago during a severe
earthquake which visited southern California.

At last the mighty roar of the Yosemite fell
upon our ears, and looking across the valley we
beheld the object of our trip. As we drove on
the roar became like the roar of distant thunder,
approaching nearer and nearer as we advanced.

Driving up to the Stoneman House and going
to register our names we encountered a hotel
clerk who was so sublimely impudent as to merit
passing notice here. So arrogant was he that
our party would have left and taken quarters
elsewhere had it been possible to do so. This
self-important individual was the son of the
proprietor of the hotel, Mr. Cook (who, by the

way, was very unlike the young man, and was manager of the stage line when not engaged in making himself generally obnoxious in his capacity as clerk. We had occasion to severely speak our minds to him on more than one occasion before leaving, and it was only after threatening him that we were able to secure seats in the stage leaving the day we desired. He assigned us the worst places, and tried to put us to as much inconvenience as possible by attempting to separate our party. It was evident that he was provoked because we would not stay and help eat the spoiled meats and poorly-cooked vegetables that were served to his guests.

After we had reluctantly partaken of a meal of putrid meats and chicken broth, with some poorly-cooked beans, two of us started to walk to the Yosemite Falls. It was a pleasant stroll of a couple of miles. We followed the wagon-trail for some distance and then cut across the meadow-land and followed up the Yosemite creek, which is fed by the waters from the falls and empties into the Merced river. The force of the water striking the rocks at the foot of the lower falls drove clouds of mist and spray from the cañon as if forced out by a hurricane. It

was like facing a driving rain-storm to get where
we could secure a good view of the falls, and
we had to give it up.   Our clothes were soaking
wet, and we retired somewhat discomfited at not
being able to accomplish our desire.   The roar
of the falling waters is something awful, and
can be heard in almost every portion of the
valley.   The falls are on the northern wall of
the valley, and are seen from the verandas of
both hotels.   They are said to be the grandest
and most sublime waterfalls in the world.   The
distance from where the waters take their first
plunge until they reach the Merced river is about
2,550 feet.   There are, however, three distinct
falls—the upper, middle and lower   The distance from the brink of the upper falls to the
middle is an unbroken plunge of about 1,500
feet.   It is said that there is no other waterfall
yet discovered carrying so great a volume of
water from such a height.   The middle portion is a series of cascades with a descent of 625
feet, and the lower fall is another direct plunge
of 400 feet.   As we were in the valley early in
the season, the volume of water coming over the
precipice was enormous.   As the snow gradually
melts and is carried off the amount of water becomes appreciably less, and during the latter part

of the season it is said that one can approach quite near the falls and with safety pass under the upper fall.

In returning to the hotel we walked along the banks of the beautiful Merced river. The water was as clear as crystal, and occasionally a trout was seen darting here and there among the rocks, or basking in the sunshine. We passed several Indian huts and noticed a number of peculiar-looking objects about the size of flour barrels, made of boughs and stuck upon poles about ten feet above the ground. We afterwards ascertained that they were a kind of a "cache" in which the Indians kept their winter supply of acorns. Arriving at the hotel, some of our party who had not been informed of our whereabouts were worried for fear that we had climbed one of the trails that lead up the different mountains and were unable to retrace our steps.

Sitting on the verandas we could see most of prominent peaks in the valley. The hotel stands almost at the base of the mountain upon which Glacier Point is located. There is a hotel there, and in the evening the proprietor entertained the guests of the Stoneman House by a primitive display of fireworks, which consisted of throwing burning brands over the cliff into the valley.

Back of the hotel stands Half Dome, whose summit appears to have been chiseled by some mighty power to resemble a dome, one half of which, having been dislodged by a violent convulsion of Nature, lies a mass of ruins at the foot of the mountain, leaving a perfect half dome clearly outlined, on this occasion, against a beautiful blue sky. The melting snows of centuries have polished its summit so that the dome glistens like silver when the first rays of the morning sun make their appearance in the east. Cloud's Rest is another mountain whose summit penetrates the clouds. It is one of the points to visit, and to reach it requires some effort and considerable climbing. Directly opposite Glacier Point are the Royal Arches and the Royal Arch Falls. In front of the hotel are all the peaks and points passed while entering the valley.

It being early in the season and the snow still deep on the mountains, numerous waterfalls were to be seen on all sides. Many of them have not been named from the fact that they dry up long before the season closes, and in fact some of them disappear in a few weeks after the season opens.

After a refreshing sleep we were ready in the morning to put in a whole day exploring the valley. The first thing on our programme was to visit Mirror Lake and see the sun rise. Some of the party took stages, but two of us concluded to walk, as we did not have to be there until nine o'clock, as the sun did not appear above the tops of the mountains until that time. On the way we met a gentleman who very kindly offered to show us the route, and, thinking that he was well acquainted with the way, we followed him. After walking about half an hour we came upon a party of campers consisting of two young married couples who were out for a two weeks' stay in the woods and were prepared for roughing it. The ladies were dressed in suits made of bed ticking, with short skirts and heavy shoes. We chatted with them for a few moments and found that we were on the wrong trail and had farther to go to reach the lake than before leaving the hotel. Consequently we were unable to reach the lake before the rest of our party had left, and not until after the sun had risen. We lingered along its banks, and gazing upon it saw every cloud in the sky, every mountain, crag and peak, and every tree and bush near its edge faithfully reflected in the crystal water at our feet. The birds and insects that flitted across were distinctly seen upon its mirror-like surface.

Returning to the hotel we spent the time before dinner buying views and resting on the verandas. Going into the dining-room we ascertained that the chicken broth of the previous dinner had not all been disposed of, so what was left was diluted with water and served as chicken soup. The chickens came on at the next meal.

Soon after, a carriage that had been ordered the evening before drove up. We took our seats and started on "The Grand Tour" of the valley. The road led us along the banks of the Merced river, and we were entertained by the driver, who had an unlimited supply of interesting legends to relate. Every prominent crag and point had its story. As we passed grand old El Capitan, with its polished sides glistening in the afternoon sun, he pointed out in a cleft over half-way up its side a tree said to be over one hundred and twenty-five feet in height, although, from our point of view, it looked like a small shrub. He also pointed out a discoloration in the rock having a strong resemblance to a man's head, from which the rock takes its name, "El Capitan," the captain. Following the course of the river we soon came to the only private grounds within the valley. It is a claim taken by a prospector before the park was set aside by the United States Government as a national pleasure-ground. There is a deserted shanty, upon the door of which many tourists have inscribed their names. The place used to be a favorite drive for tourists who wished to get a good meal of trout, and no doubt it was very popular, judging from the fare we received at the hotel. The road now runs along the banks of the river, and in several places the rocks had to be blasted in order to clear an opening for the driveway. In the river are numerous large boulders which have rolled down the mountain sides, and choking the stream have formed a series of rapids which are very beautiful and add much to the romantic surroundings. The road now became very narrow, and we were congratulating ourselves that there were no carriages coming in the opposite direction, as there would be difficulty in passing, when we were startled by the driver shouting "Look out there! Hold up!" and looking ahead we saw a small buggy approaching. In it were a couple of young folks returning from the lower end of the valley. In trying to make room for our team to pass they came very near being thrown over the bank into the rushing waters of the rapids. As it was

they were only saved by the presence-of-mind
of the young lady.

At the lower end of the valley are the Cascades, a series of falls not so high as those we
had just passed, but considerably more broken
We spent some time trying to get near them,
but on account of the clouds of mist that were
being driven from the cañon by the wind, we
were compelled to give it up, and started on
the return to the hotel.   Retracing our steps
we crossed the river, and, following the road,
came to a spring of water which the driver
wished all to taste, as it was so clear and cold.
Near this spot, the driver said, the bones of two
white men were found soon after the discovery
of the valley.   They were supposed to have
been prospectors who had wandered into the
valley and been killed by the Indians, as an
arrow point was found imbedded in the skull
of one of them.   It was about four o'clock when
we drove up to the Bridal Veil Falls, where we
witnessed a most wonderful rainbow.   The position of the sun in the west shining upon the
clouds of spray and mist formed a sight singu-
larly beautiful.   We were allowed some time to
gaze upon this wonderful scene, and all left it
with reluctance.

As we drove toward the hotel the driver called our attention to a beautiful ribbon like waterfall which appeared to dissolve itself into mist before reaching the base of the cliff. He told us that it was named the "Widow's Tears," from the fact that it "dried up in six weeks." A little farther on we passed a couple of men returning from a ride up one of the trails, and the figures cut by them were most comical. They were both astride burros, and being above the average height they were compelled to sit in an uncomfortable position to keep their feet from dragging along the ground. They were accompanied by an ancient specimen of humanity who, from his antiquated dress and flowing white beard, would be easily mistaken for "Rip Van Winkle." As we drove up, the little animals seemed sleepy enough, but we had not proceeded far before we heard a scampering behind us, and, looking back, saw our two friends coming up the road at a furious rate. They dashed past us, hauling and pulling on the reins, but to no effect—the donkeys had heard the call for supper and were bound for the stable, and nothing could stop them.

Reaching the hotel we were somewhat tired, but fully repaid for the trouble we had taken to get into the valley. The charming sights of the day had surpassed all expectation. The evening was spent upon the piazzas, where we sat looking across the valley at the majestic Yosemite Falls. We retired early in order that we might be fully rested for the rough riding of the next two days. The roar of the Yosemite lulled us to sleep, from which we were aroused in the morning by a knock upon our doors and the an-anouncement that it was time to arise if we wished to take the stage for Wawona.

At seven o'clock we were seated in the stage ready to start. As we drove down past Barnard's we observed a little church nestled among the trees, showing that the spiritual welfare of tourists was not overlooked. Soon a turn in the road shut the Yosemite Falls from our view, but the roar followed us until we commenced the ascent of the zigzag road leading up the wall of the valley to Inspiration Point. We passed the Widow's Tears, then the Bridal Veil, and looking across the valley took a last glance at the Maiden's Tears. Grand El Capitan, standing out like a buttress to guard the valley, was ever before us until we turned our backs upon him at Inspiration Point, where we drove into the woods and lost sight of the valley, its peaks, domes and waterfalls. Arriving at Inspiration Point, we were allowed to take a farewell view of the valley while the horses were given a breathing spell The time passed rapidly, when the driver, cracking his whip, started the horses off on a gallop after the stages which had preceded us.

Since entering the valley the roads had not improved, and we were bounced from one side of the stage to the other in a frightful and most ridiculous manner. A lady occupying the back seat with her husband was thrown with great force against the seat in front, and came near fainting. As we drove along the road past deep snow-drifts, several of the party got out and secured snow-plants. They are in form somewhat like an asparagus-plant, though much larger, the stalk being as thick as a man's wrist, and the color is of the deepest red. They are found along the edges of the snow-drifts, pushing their heads up through the ground as soon as the frost fairly gets out of it.

An important fact seldom stated in cold type is that women, when they visit this valley and wish to thoroughly explore the wonders of the Yosemite, must use the donkeys to carry them over the rough mountain trails, and must ride astride. Sometimes, when ascending the side of a mountain, the trail is so steep that a woman, if perched sideways, would surely come to grief; and on a trail where an accident means a probable fall of a thousand feet or more, the reason for thus riding is apparent. Women must either forego the wonders of the Yosemite or discard the side-saddle while in the valley.

It was dinner-time when we drove up to Major Washburn's hotel at Wawona, where we had left one of our party a few days before while we made the trip to the valley. She had been under the care of Major Washburn's family, who had made her stay a most pleasant one, and she was ready to start with us in the morning for Raymond, where we were once more to enter the cars.

After a first-class meal, which we all appreciated, the stages drove up and we started for an afternoon's ride to the Mariposa Grove of big trees. The distance covered during the afternoon was about eighteen miles.

The road wound around the mountains, gradually ascending until we reached an altitude of over 5,000 feet. The trees first seen were in what is known as the lower grove, but they were not so large as those farther up the mountain. Reaching the "Grizzly Giant," the driver stopped his horses and many of us got out and walked around this monarch of the forest. A number of Raymond excursionists had Kodaks, and quite a number of snap shots were taken of the tree. The "Giant" is over thirty feet in diameter and more than ninety feet in circumference The first branches are over one hundred feet from the ground and measure six feet in diameter. A drive of a mile brought us to the upper grove, where over 350 trees are standing. Many of them have a brass, marble or iron plate fastened in the bark, upon which is inscribed the name given to each particular tree. The road, in making the circuit of the grove, passes through a living tree. When we passed through it the driver halted for a moment to show us how large the "tunnel" was. Two horses and the entire stage were covered by the arch. We then drove to the centre of the grove, where the keeper has his lodge. He adds considerable to his salary by selling to tourists pieces of bark cut into fancy shapes. Near his cabin is the "Fallen Giant," one of the trees which has fallen. In course of time it will no doubt be carried away by tourists who cut pieces from it.

On the return to the hotel we passed a couple of drunken Indians. They were trying to mount a small pony, but, being under the influence of liquor, they cut a very sorry figure. They fell off quite a number of times, and had it not been for that kind Providence which sometimes strangely attends fools, drunken men and children, they would have broken their necks. As domestic horses are very restive when in the presence of Indians, it was with great difficulty that we passed them. Two men had to get out and take the leaders by the bits and guide them past the drunken red men. The stages following us had a more exciting time. The Indians, having mounted the pony, came down the mountain like a whirlwind, leaping stones and fallen trees and yelling like demons. The stage-horses reared and plunged, and it required the utmost skill of the drivers to prevent a serious accident.

The best supper we had eaten since leaving Grant's Springs, as we entered the valley, was awaiting us upon our arrival at the hotel. Major Washburn and his family understand the art of keeping a hotel, and many of the travelers coming from the valley remain several days at his comfortable hostelry.

At seven o'clock in the morning the stages drove up to the hotel, and passengers for

Raymond soon filled them. It was our fortune again to be passengers in the stage with Ed. Crawford, the accommodating driver who had brought us from Raymond when we entered the valley, and who had explained so much of interest to us. Our stage was next to the last that left Wawona, but as we stopped at the relays our team was gradually moved up front, and at Grub Gulch we took the lead, which we kept. Crawford, by a series of manœuvres, had secured the United States mail, and that gave us preference as to right of way.

After leaving Grub Gulch we noticed in the valley below us a large trough winding along the base of the mountain. It was filled with running water. Crawford explained that it was used by the saw-mill operators up in the mountains for running their lumber down to the railroad. The water in the trough was supplied from mountain brooks, and the lumber placed in the trough at the mill would float down to the end of the trough, where it would be placed on the cars or stacked up to dry. The "canal," as he termed it, was about fifty miles long, and as lumber was cheap it was constructed at a comparatively small cost, and was the cheapest and most convenient method of transportation.

The roads which, when we entered the valley, were mud, had now become dust. The horses, as they moved along, left clouds of it in their wake, which we breathed to our great discom-fort. Occasionally a gust of wind would drive the clouds from us, and during the breathing spell we would look back to see how far the coming stages were behind us. Their position was easily discerned from the clouds of dust that followed them.

When we came within sight of Raymond and the steam cars, the passengers gave a shout which made the mountains ring. We were at last within sight of the end of our jolting and hard riding. The occupants of each stage gave vent to their feelings in the same manner. We congratulated ourselves, our driver and every-body else that all had returned from the valley alive and were able to continue the journey.

Bidding good-bye to Crawford, we went into the hotel and ate a fairly good supper, and then proceeded to the sleeping-cars which had been engaged before leaving the valley. When we entered our sleeper the thermometer registered ninety-two, and we made up our minds that sleep was out of the question. We were very agreeably disappointed in this matter, for when the train started, a draft was made through the cars which soon cooled them off, and we sank into peaceful slumbers.

It was noon, Sunday, when we crossed the beautiful San Francisco Bay on our return to the city. We were soon back in our old quarters at the Palace Hotel. Going into the corridor we were most agreeably surprised at meeting seventeen of our party who had made the trip across the continent.

In the evening an impromptu reception was held in the parlors of the hotel, where all of the party met and passed several hours most agreeably. Some had made arrangements to continue their trip to Alaska, and were anxious that the rest of us should accompany them and keep the party intact as long as possible. As none of the ladies of the party had visited Chinatown by night it was determined to make another trip to that locality Monday evening. Colonel Thompson was deputized to make the arrangements, and at a late hour we adjourned to our sleeping-apartments to meet in the parlors Monday evening at seven o'clock, where a guide was to be in waiting.

Chapter IV.

California Resorts.

On the eighth day of October, 1776, while the inhabitants of the eastern shore of what is now the United States were engaged in a warfare to throw off the oppressive yoke of a foreign country and establish a nation of their own, a number of Spanish monks, having pushed their way up along the coast of what is now the Golden State of the Union, established one of their missions on the ground upon which the magnificent city of San Francisco now stands.

Under the fostering care of this mission a village bearing the name of Yerba Buena was established. This was in 1835, almost sixty years after the monks first visited the place. The village received this somewhat singular name from the fact that a medicinal herb called "yerba buena" grew in great abundance on the site. It is Spanish, and means "good herb."

The old mission building is still standing, and is used as a place of worship. The building is of adobe, and the walls are three feet thick.

The floor is of earth, and the roof is covered with heavy tiling. Clustered around the mission are the old adobe buildings once occupied by the monks, who sought, by their pretended sacrifices, to improve the spiritual condition of the Indians, and also to live upon the fat of the land. These buildings are all in a dilapidated condition. The old mission burying-ground adjoins the building. Most of the inscriptions on the tombs are in Spanish, and were not decipherable by us.

The name of San Francisco was given to the place in 1847, and from that time forward the town commenced to grow. It was the principal city in the State as soon as gold was discovered, and from here all expeditions were made into the diggings. During the "fifties" it was a rendezvous for all the cut-throats and gamblers who could get here. This class of citizens became so bold in their operations that in 1856 the famous Vigilance Committee was organized, and some of the most notorious of them were executed and a number banished. This method of treatment terrorized the tough element, and the town became tranquil and one of the most orderly in the country.

The city in its earlier days was a great sufferer
from fires, there having been six great confla-
grations during the two years beginning December 24th, 1849, and ending June 22d, 1851. The
amount of property destroyed in that time was
over $26,500,000.

Thoroughly refreshed by a full night's rest,
we gladly welcomed Monday morning. Our
rooms were located on the third floor of the
Palace Hotel and faced the inner court. Consequently we were not disturbed by the continuous clanging of the gongs of the street cars
that traverse all sections of the city, and pass
the hotel on their way to the wharf two or three
squares below. Breakfast over, we took a street
car and were soon on our way to Golden Gate
Park, the principal pleasure-ground of the city.
The car landed us at the main entrance, and
soon a carriage was engaged for a drive through
the park and out to the Cliff House. The time
spent in the park was most enjoyable, and the
display of flowers was remarkable. There
seemed to be an endless variety, and before we
left the grounds we were almost bewildered by
them. In the Horticultural building was seen
one of the few specimens of the Victoria Regia

lily in the United States. The driveway led us
past the immense music-stand where, every
Sunday afternoon, concerts are given by the
finest band in the city. Near by is a monument
erected to the memory of President Garfield.

Passing out of the park we were soon traveling
over a macadamized road, cut through the sand
dunes, on our way to the famous Cliff House.
Reaching the ocean the road followed the contour of the beach for some distance and then
wound around the cliff until we reached our
destination. Along the beach were groups of
children wading and splashing in the water and
evidently enjoying themselves to the greatest
extent. Our driver drew up rein at the door
of the Cliff House and we all dismounted and
went inside. Being near the noon hour, we ate
luncheon and then went out upon the pavilion
to view the seals and seal-rocks. The rocks
upon which the seals bask are about a quarter
of a mile from shore, and opera-glasses were
procured at the refreshment stand to assist in
the novel view. Long before we reached the
Cliff House the dismal bellowing of the seals
could be heard. Hundreds of the animals were
seen sunning themselves upon the rocks or
swimming around them. Upon one of the

smaller rocks two large seals were fighting apparently for the mastery of it and the favor of the female seals near them. The contest did not last long before one of them was driven into the water. The victor then gave a series of bellows, as if to challenge any one of his rivals to a combat. His notes were answered by an immense seal named "Ben Butler" that was sunning himself on the top of the highest rock. As he rushed down the rock at a furious rate, many of the seals in their haste to get out of his way flopped over into the ocean. He bellowed continuously, and, reaching the water, plunged in and started direct for his rival. As he approached the rock the other was ready for him and he was kept in the water for some time, but finally getting a hold with his flippers he clambered up on the rock. The battle did not last long before "Ben" had driven his rival into the water, and was once more looked upon by the females as the undisputed champion.

We lingered some time watching the antics of the seals and then started on the return trip to the city. We drove to Sutro's Park, which overlooks the Cliff House, and walked through it. Near the house were chained a couple of bears and a monkey. The mischievous monkey

was continually worrying the bears by trying
to steal some of the food which the latter were
eating. It would get up as close as it dared
and then chatter at a furious rate. If any move
was made by the bears the monkey would be
up one of the near-by trees in an instant. We
watched the antics of this mischievous creature
for some time, and then strolled through the
labyrinth of flowers back to the gate where our
carriage was awaiting us. Returning to the
city we drove past the presidio, or the fort,
which commands the Golden Gate or entrance
to San Francisco Bay.

It was dinner time when we arrived at the
hotel. By chance we met the entire party in the
corridors, and as we walked to the dining-room
we organized a trip to Chinatown for the benefit
of the ladies, who were left behind on the former
trip. While waiting in the parlor after supper
for the different members to assemble, Mr. George
W. Childs, of the *Public Ledger*, Philadelphia,
came in, and as some of the party were acquainted with Mr. Childs, we were each in turn
presented to him. He was very agreeable, of
course, and showed us a couple of handsome
screens which had been presented to him by

some young lady at one of the towns where his party had stopped.

Everything being in readiness, we selected Colonel Thompson as leader and off we started. Our guide was very loquacious, and answered innumerable questions put to him by the lady members of the party. In going to our destination we avoided Dupont street and entered by way of Portsmouth Square. This square, during the gold fever, fronted on the bay, but now there are several blocks of large buildings between it and the wharves. We visited many of the stores and clambered through underground passages, going in one building and out another We visited the theatre, but as there was no performance going on the ladies were somewhat disappointed. We visited the restaurant connected with the theatre, but had to hurry through because one of the young ladies became faint when she saw the manner in which the food was being prepared. Going into the theatre, we prevailed upon one of the parties in charge to show us some of the costumes worn by the actors. They were gorgeous, being worked with gold lace and bullion. The weight of some of them would soon tire a person out if worn for any length of time. Passing up and down some of the streets we would frequently hear the discordant screeching of one of the favorite musical instruments of the Chinese, accompanied by the din of clanging cymbals. Every now and then we would hear the explosion of firecrackers in some of the houses. We entered one of the many restaurants, and, going up-stairs, saw a Chinese banquet in progress. The guests were few and were outnumbered by the musicians. They were sitting around on ebony stools inlaid with mother-of-pearl. The men and the women were evidently filled with wine, as some of the former were quite lively and others were lying with their heads in the laps of the women We were not allowed in the room, but saw all we wished to see from the balcony, which was built along the outside of the building.

Returning to the street, we next visited one of the Joss-houses and bought more of the incense-sticks to "bling gooda luck." From here we went to the largest and most expensive restaurant within the confines of Chinatown. Mounting two flights of steps we entered a room, the furniture of which was either solid mahogany or ebony inlaid with mother-of-pearl. The draperies and other furnishings of the rooms were on the same expensive scale. We all gathered

around one of the handsome tables and sipped
our tea and ate Chinese sweetmeats until we
started for the hotel, where we arrived thoroughly tired out.

Having rested well during the night, we determined in the morning to visit San Rafael, one of
the suburban towns, where many of San Francisco's wealthy citizens built their homes in order
to be out of the din and noise of a bustling city.
It is on the western shore of San Pablo Bay, fifteen miles from the great metropolis　It takes its
name from one of the old missions formerly
located there　The mission has been destroyed,
and in its place are pleasant homes.　To realize
that the place is healthy, one only has to see the
numerous ruddy-faced children of all ages that
abound in every door-yard.

Our vacation was getting shorter and shorter
every day, and in order to visit all of the places
we contemplated it was necessary that our stay
in San Francisco should be shortened and that
we proceed upon our trip to Menlo Park, San
José, Santa Cruz and Monterey. Leaving the
city by one of the early trains, we passed
through a section of the suburbs given over to
Chinese residents for truck-farms. The plots
were not very large, but each one had its wind-

mill for pumping water for irrigation. There
were hundreds of them, reminding one of pictures of Holland. The country through which
we passed was very fertile, and the fields of growing grain were beautiful to look upon.

The train halted at a neat little station and the
conductor called, "All out for Menlo Park."
Near this place is the Leland Stanford, Jr., University. It is the gift of Senator Stanford, and
stands as a monument to the memory of his only
son, Leland Stanford, Jr., who died in 1884. It
is endowed to the extent of twenty millions of
dollars. The buildings are erected on the Palo
Alto Farm, which consists of over seven thousand acres. It is the home of Senator Stanford,
and here are also located his famous breeding-
stables. Hiring a carriage we were taken out to
the University. It is of Moorish design and
encloses an immense quadrangle. The buildings
are mostly one story in height and covered with
red tiling. The dormitories are several stories in
height and are located on either side of the University. Within the quadrangle a continuous
colonnade connects all the buildings. The art
museum and the library buildings are located in
front of the main building, a little to the right.

From the University grounds we were taken to
the stables, and had the pleasure of seeing the
famous trotter, Palo Alto, exercised.   There were
quite a number of horses in the stables, and we
spent some time watching the different trainers
take them out and give them their daily exercise
around the track.

Returning to the station, we were soon upon
our way to San José.   This latter place is the
county seat of Santa Clara county, and is called
the "Garden City of the World."   We arrived
here early in the afternoon and went direct to
Hotel Vendome.   As is the case with all sight-
seers, before we were fully settled in our rooms
we had ordered a carriage for a drive through
the town and over to Santa Clara, a small village
that has grown up under the fostering care of
one of the old missions that was established in
1777.   Connecting the two cities is a magnificent
driveway known as the Alameda.   The willows
and pepper trees which line it on both sides were
planted by the Indian converts, under the supervision of the Jesuit Fathers, who lived in the
mission.   The distance between the two places
being only three miles, Santa Clara was soon
reached.   The old mission church is still standing, and is used as a place of worship.   Like all

the buildings erected by the Spaniards, it is of adobe, and is showing the ravages of time. In front of the church is an old cross, erected by the Indian converts soon after the mission was founded. It is now encased in a wooden frame, excepting the front, which is glass, so that the cross may be seen by all who pass by. Within the enclosure surrounding the mission is the Santa Clara College, under the discipline of the Roman Catholic Church. It is one of the best colleges under the control of that church in the State. On our return to San José we passed the grounds of the University of the Pacific, one of the strongest colleges on the Pacific coast. It is under the jurisdiction of the Methodist Episcopal Church, and ranks high as an educational institution.

The country tributary to San José is very fertile, and fruit-growing is the principal industry. Prunes, raisins and other dried and canned fruits are shipped in large quantities from this place. Lick Observatory is located on the summit of Mount Hamilton, twenty-six miles away. Stages leave the hotel every morning, and occupy the entire day going to and returning from the observatory. At eight o'clock in the morning the stage drove up to the door and our party,

now decreased to five, took seats in it and
started.   For some distance both sides of the
road was shaded with rows of eucalyptus trees,
and the perfume from their blossoms filled the
air.   Reaching the foot hills we commenced the
ascent of the mountains, which consumed the
entire forenoon.   As we gradually rose from the
plain the valley lay spread out below us.   The
orchards and vineyards, clad in their garments of
green, made a most beautiful picture.   Before
reaching the dinner station we changed horses
twice, and were enabled to make good time.
The road, unlike the one entering the Yosemite
Valley, was almost as level as a floor, and we
were not subjected to such a shaking-up as we
received when we entered and departed from the
latter place.   The road cost the county of Santa
Clara almost $100,000.   Arriving at the dinner-
station we were within two miles of the observa·
tory, in a direct line, but as we had to follow the
road we were still seven miles from our destination.   This road was constructed upon methods
suggested by the donor of the great observatory,
Mr. James Lick.   It is seven miles long, one
mile for each day of the week; there are three
hundred and sixty-five turns, one for every day
in the year; and at one point twelve divisions of

the road are to be seen, one to represent each
month in the year.

On arriving at the observatory everybody was
requested to register in a book kept for that purpose, after which, in company with the janitor,
we made a circuit of the buildings and were
taken to the room in which the large telescope is
kept. Under the foundation upon which the
large instrument is erected lie the remains of Mr.
Lick The janitor gave us a short history of the
institution and everybody connected with it. He
had learned his piece by heart, and repeated it to
every stage-load of people who came to see the
place, and will probably continue to tell the same
story, in the same words, as long as he holds his
position.

When we had made a tour of all the rooms we
were escorted by one of the professors to the
cupola in which the small telescope is kept, and
pointing it at one of the stars he permitted us to
look through the instrument

The return trip was very pleasant. While
passing a hill upon which a great number of
ground-squirrels were seen, the driver espied a
coyote on the lookout for a squirrel with which
to make an evening meal. As the party had no
firearms with them he was permitted to stand

there unmolested. It was early in the evening when we reached the hotel, and some of us walked down the Alameda towards Santa Clara before supper.

Bidding farewell to lovely San José, we took the train for Los Gatos. It was but a short run of nine miles, and we were soon at our destination. The town has about two thousand inhabitants and is nestled in the Santa Cruz mountains, overlooking the beautiful and fertile valley of Santa Clara of the North. Like San José it is the centre of a fruit growing section, and upon the hills and mountain sides are to be seen the well-kept vineyards and orchards. The first cherries of the season were just coming in when we reached the little town.

Some of our party went direct to the ranch of a friend, while the remainder put up at the hotel. We had scarcely become settled in our apartments when a carriage drove up to the door and in it were two young ladies and their father, who had come to take us carriage-riding around the country and over the hills. The whole afternoon was spent in the carriage, and as the road wound around the mountains some most enchanting views of the valley were had.

Returning to the hotel we were invited to spend the evening at the ranch of our friend. It is within the corporate limits of the town, and upon it are bearing orchards of apricots, cherries, English walnuts, and a vineyard. We feasted upon cherries, and during our stay in the town visited his cherry-orchard many times. Our visit to Los Gatos will long be pleasantly remembered.

It was Decoration Day when we left for Santa Cruz and Monterey. When we arrived at the station our friends were already there, and in their arms were several large bags of excellent cherries. A charming auburn-haired young lady presented the writer with a bagful, remarking that she had picked them herself especially for him. This, of course, was pleasing, adding extra flavor to the fruit, and may the memory of the auburn-haired young lady and the cherries never be obliterated.

Before the train pulled into the station the Grand Army men and the different societies of the town were forming in the square in front of the station for the parade. One club, known as the " Jags," had a membership of about thirty-five, and each one carried a Japanese parasol. They were patients at the Keely Institute located

in Los Gatos.   On account of this institute the
pretty town is often referred to as " Jag Town."

The ride over the Santa Cruz mountains was
most enjoyable.   The railroad passes quite near
the Santa Cruz grove of big trees, and we could
see them from the car windows.   At Santa Cruz
we drove out to the cliffs, where the action of the
waves has cut the bluff into all sorts of fantastic
forms.   We also drove along the beach where the
bath-houses are located and saw the crowds of
bathers plunging in the surf.

Wishing to spend all the time practicable at
the Hotel Del Monte, at Monterey, we took the
earliest train leaving Santa Cruz for the latter
place.   It was but a short ride through a beautiful country to the station of Del Monte, located
within the park surrounding the hotel.   The
road leading to the hotel is as level as a floor,
and winds in and out among the gnarled live-
oaks and pines of great size and incalculable age.
When we registered and were being shown to
our rooms, we unexpectedly met in the corridors
six members of our original "Golden Gate"
party.   They had been here for several days,
and were awaiting advice from San Francisco as
to whether they could secure accommodations on
the steamer "Queen," which was to sail from

Tacoma, Washington, on the sixth day of June, for Alaska. It was a pleasant reunion, and during our stay in Del Monte we were together most of the time.

Surrounding the hotel is a park of one hundred and twenty-six acres, all under the care of a head gardener and numerous assistants. Flowers of almost every variety bloom in profusion. In some places the underbrush has not been cleared out, and the forest in its natural state forms a pleasing contrast to the well-kept lawns and flower-beds to be seen upon every side. The "Arizona Garden" is composed of many varieties of cacti, which thrive in the balmy air of lovely Monterey.

To visit Del Monte and not take the "Eighteen-Mile Drive" would be to miss one of the most pleasing features of the place. It was early in the afternoon when the stage, drawn by four handsome bays, was driven up to the hotel, and our party took seats within. It seemed a short drive through avenues lined on either side with pines and cedars until we left the confines of the park and approached the quaint old town of Monterey. In 1602 one of the early Spanish navigators, Don Sebastian Vizcaino, entered Monterey Bay, and landing with a couple of

Hotel Del Monte, Monterey, California.

priests and a company of soldiers took possession of the country in the name of the Spanish king. According to the custom of the Spaniards of that day, a cross was erected and an altar built under one of the trees, and mass was celebrated. The commander of the expedition did not remain very long, but taking his priests and soldiers aboard his ships returned to Mexico. For one hundred and sixty-eight years it retained its primitive silence, when, in 1770, Father Junipero Serra, the leader of a band of Franciscan missionaries, landed at Monterey and established the Mission de San Carlos de Monterey. The friars immediately set about converting the Indians to Christianity and then making slaves of the newly-fledged Christians, whom they set to work tilling the soil and tending the herds of cattle and droves of swine. In the latter part of 1771, by order of the Marquis de Croix, the mission was removed to Carmelo valley, about five miles south of Monterey. Within the walls of the latter mission lie the remains of Father Junipero Serra and three of his most intimate followers. The presidio was left at Monterey, and within its enclosure is the present antiquated Roman Catholic church. Following the zigzag street, we came to the old fort, built upon one of the hills

overlooking the bay. The ramparts are easily
traced, and some of the old guns, formidable in
their time, looked down upon us. On an emi-
nence near the fort stands a statue of Father
Junipero Serra, erected by Mrs Senator Stanford
in commemoration of the work done by the old
friar.

The history of Monterey and Monterey county
is most interesting reading, and tells of the rise
and decline of the quaint old town. The old
missions come in for a great deal of mention, and
their downfall is sad to read. In 1813 they had
reached the zenith of their power and wealth,
and from that time commenced to decline. The
Spanish government despoiled them of much of
their riches, and after the independence of Mexico was secured that nation confiscated what was
left, and the old missions became deserted. Of
late years, however, the old buildings have been
restored and are now occupied as places of worship. In spite of the many vicissitudes of the
missions, Monterey flourished until 1847, when
it was the principal town in the State and the
seat of government. With the rise of San Francisco and the removal of the seat of government
to San José its decline was rapid, and it has
never been able to regain its former supremacy.

A short distance from Monterey is Pacific Grove, the great Methodist camp-ground of the Pacific States. It is to the Pacific Slope what Ocean Grove and Cottage City are to the Eastern States. Passing through the main avenue of the place we noticed many beautiful cottages and a large hotel. The auditorium is not so large as the one at Ocean Grove, but it is yet strikingly large. From Pacific Grove the road leaves the beach and turns inland, and passing through Point Pinos Rancho we came to the Pacific ocean at Moss Beach. In among the rocks a number of Chinese have put up some rude shanties to protect them from the elements. They make their living by catching fish and selling shells to the tourists who pass along the road. Several of them were squatting alongside their little heaps of shells and star-fish, eager to sell us specimens at much lower prices than we could purchase at the curio-stores of the town. Like San Francisco, Monterey has its seal-rocks. They are on the eighteen-mile drive, near Cypress Point. There were hundreds of seals basking in the sunshine or swimming around the rocks, some of them quite near the shore. There is a heavy penalty against shooting at them. After leaving the seal-rocks we came to the wonderful grove of Monterey cypress. The trees are gnarled and twisted into various shapes, and their flat tops give them the form of an immense umbrella. This is the only place where they are known to exist. Dante, in writing his "Inferno," must have dreamed of the Monterey cypress. Some of them are able to derive sustenance from the bare rocks over which the roots sprawl and grasp with fierce tenacity. We were taken out on Cypress Point, where the driver, stopping his horses to allow us to take in the view, calmly remarked that five bays could be seen from this point. After a fruitless effort to see more than one, he pointed to his team of four bays, which made up the five. Driving on we passed several Chinese with piles of shells in front of them and numbers of bright pebbles from Pebble Beach. At Pescadero Beach we turned into the forests of pine and oak. The road wound in and out of shady ravines, and, gradually ascending, reached the crest of a ridge which terminates in Cypress Point. Looking back, a view of surpassing beauty greeted our vision. Carmelo bay, with its waters of dark blue, tranquil and smooth, reminds one of the fairy scenes of childhood.

The road now leads us back through Monterey, and we are soon at the hotel ready for dinner. While we were gone a telegram was received by our friends, stating that accommodations had been secured for them in the steamer "Queen," and that they must answer at once whether or not they would accept. It did not take them long to decide, and the accommodations were secured.

Our stay at Del Monte was necessarily brief, as we had to make our preparations and be in Tacoma by June 5th and claim our state-rooms.

During the afternoon we visited the Maze and tried to thread its treacherous paths, and in the evening we visited the club house and walked through the grounds.

CHAPTER V.

ALASKA.

Totem-Pole, Fort Wrangle.

TO COME across the continent and return without visiting Alaska is a great mistake. The voyage is in a large ocean steamer, unaccompanied by the usual sea-sickness that goes with a trip across the Atlantic or Pacific oceans. After you have made up your mind to go, make your arrangements if possible to go by the steamer "Queen," and you will never regret it. We had almost given up the idea that we could secure berths on the steamer that was to leave Tacoma June 6th, and were preparing to commence our homeward trip, when a telegram was received stating that state-rooms had been secured, and to come and claim them immediately. There was a hurried repacking of trunks, accompanied with the usual excitement preparatory to taking a new trip. Heavy wraps were brought up from the bottom of the trunks and put in convenient places and everything gotten ready for a trip to the Land of Glaciers.

We left Monterey early in the afternoon, reaching San Francisco before night. The following morning was devoted to securing our steamer tickets and making a few necessary purchases. The afternoon was over half spent when our party, now increased to nine by the arrival of the four Pittsburg ladies, met in the ferry-house at the foot of Market street and were soon on board the ferry-boat bound for Oakland, where we were to take the cars. It was a beautiful sight as we beheld the vessels of every nation lying at anchor either in the bay or along the wharves of the great western metropolis. The sun was just sinking behind the hills of San Francisco when we entered the ferry-house at Oakland, and the reflection of its rays on the window-panes gave one the impression that an immense conflagration was raging on every hill-top. Before leaving Oakland several beautiful bouquets of fragrant flowers were presented to the lady members of the party.

The distance from San Francisco to Portland over the Southern Pacific Railroad is 772 miles, and the time occupied in traveling between the two cities was two nights and one day.

The scenery along the railroad is wonderfully grand. For several hours on the day after leaving San Francisco we traveled under the shadow of snow-capped Mount Shasta. At the Shasta Soda Springs the train stopped for a few moments to allow the passengers to get out and drink the refreshing waters. In the afternoon, while looking out of the car windows, we noticed that our train passed over the tracks of what we thought was some other railroad, but upon asking the brakeman where the road led to he said that in a few minutes we would be riding on those tracks, as the road, in climbing the mountain, made a complete loop and run under itself.

The next morning we arrived in Portland, where our Pittsburg friends left the train to spend the day in that city, and were to meet us in Tacoma in the evening. All forenoon we traveled through magnificent forests of stately trees. At noon we were in Tacoma, quartered at the hotel of the same name. Its location is admirable, being on a bluff overlooking Puget Sound, one of the finest harbors in the world.

At the wharves of Tacoma the vessels of the deepest draft can load and unload their cargoes without fear of being stranded at low water.

The afternoon was spent in completing arrangements for our long voyage. In the evening the parties who had stopped over in Portland arrived, and when morning came we met in the parlors of the hotel and decided as to how the intervening time until evening would be employed.

We rode on all the street-car lines in the city, and when returning to the hotel narrowly escaped being run over by a runaway horse. We were all pleased with Tacoma, and were favorably impressed with the many fine buildings which adorn the city in every section. The streets, instead of being paved, are planked, lumber being much cheaper than stone. It also has the advantage of causing less noise when the heavy wagons roll over it.

On the evening of June 5th we took possession of our state-rooms on the steamer "Queen," Captain James Carroll, commanding, and were ready for the long voyage to Muir Glacier, Sitka, and the usual stopping places *en route*.

As soon as we were shown our state-rooms and had made ourselves at home with the surround-

ings, we commenced a tour of inspection of the
floating palace that was to be our home for the
next twelve days. Our rooms opened into the
dining-room, in which were three tables, one
reaching the entire length of the room, and two
shorter ones placed in the broadest part of the
room. The social hall is on the main deck, and
is reached by a flight of steps from the dining-
room. It is well furnished with parlor furniture,
including tables for games and an upright piano.
At the stern of the vessel on the main deck is
the smoking room, where games of chess and
whist were played all day long excepting at meal
times. In the bow and stern were convenient
places for steamer chairs. The vessel was lighted
with electricity, and every convenience was at
hand.

At five o'clock Monday morning the lines were
cast off, the screw of the propeller began to churn
the water, and the trip was actually begun. Our
first stop was at Seattle, where a number of passengers came on board, among them being three
of our "Golden Gate" party, so that there were
twelve of us in the company once more. As the
boat was to remain at the wharf for some time, a
number went off and bought steamer chairs,
which came in very conveniently for lounging

when tired of promenading the deck. Near the wharf were a number of Indians living in their dug-outs, as their canoes are called. One could see nothing of the stately bearing of the "Noble Redman" so often read about. Their stature was small, to begin with, and their faces had the appearance of wrinkled leather. They were a repulsive-looking set. The expression of one of the squaws as she looked at the writer when he passed will linger with him by day and haunt him by night.

At last the whistle blew, the passengers came on board and our staunch steamer headed for the north. The shore of Puget's Sound, on each side, is densely wooded with forests of pine, fir and hemlock, beginning at the water's edge and reaching to the snow-line on the high mountains. The landscape forms a most beautiful picture of water, forest and snow-capped mountains.

Port Townsend was our next stopping-place. Here another consignment of passengers came on board. A wagon-load of mail-bags were dumped on the wharf and quickly carried on board by the deck-hands, and we availed ourselves of the opportunity to post some letters to distant friends. Everything being in readiness, the whistle blew, the gang-plank was pulled in, and the steamer

headed for Anacortes, our last landing-place in
the State of Washington. Anacortes is a small
town, with a number of very substantial buildings erected by Eastern capital. It was boomed
on paper and considerable money was invested,
but it cannot amount to much of a place, and the
investors will wait a long time before receiving
any returns for their money. Only a short stop
was made, but many of the passengers went on
shore and bought a plentiful supply of fruit and
a few souvenirs. Several passengers, owing to a
misunderstanding as to the time the steamer was
to remain at the wharf, came near getting left.
As it was, the gang-plank was hauled in, when
some one discovered them walking leisurely
down the street and informed the captain, who
ordered the plank out again and the tardy ones
came on board.

The approaches of Victoria are beautiful.
Long before we entered the harbor we saw
the prominent buildings stand out in bold relief
against an almost cloudless sky. The Dunsmuir
castle is a prominent landmark, and was seen
from far down the sound. It requires a steady
hand to navigate the intricate passage from the
outer to the inner harbor. We passed quite near
the wreck of the steamer "San Pedro," which

lay on the rocks with her bow pointing to the
sky and her stern under the water. The sun
was just setting when the steamer was made
fast to the wharf, and a most glorious sunset it
was. The gang-plank being put out, most of
the passengers availed themselves of the opportunity to set foot on English soil, and went
ashore. Quite a number of hacks and coupés

Wreck of the "San Pedro."

were there to take us around the town. Many
took street-cars, but our party secured the
services of a very intelligent driver, who took
us all over the town and pointed out everything
of interest to the tourist. There are a number
of handsome churches, which fact speaks well
for the easy-going inhabitants. The Methodists,
being the strongest, have the finest place of
worship. The Presbyterians also have a very

fine church. We were driven through Beacon Hill Park as the twilight was fading, and watched the reflection of the silver moon dancing over the rippling waters of the sound   Far away on the American shore (they always speak of the United States as "America," and the people from there as "Americans") were the flickering lights of one of the harbor towns. Our driver said that the lights were twenty miles distant. Leaving Beacon Hill we drove through the grounds of Carey Castle, the residence of the governor, and then back to the "Queen." On our way we plucked an immense bouquet of Scotch Broom for those who remained on board. We retired early in order to be up before the steamer should leave the wharf in the morning and not miss any of the beautiful scenery.

As this was our last stopping-place before entering the Alaskan boundary, several more passengers came on board and took possession of the few state-rooms that were unoccupied. There were over two hundred first class and quite a number of steerage passengers on board. The former, with but few exceptions, were tourists, while the latter were chiefly prospectors and miners going to the gold-fields of Alaska.

The boat had left her moorings and started on the way to Fort Wrangle long before the most active of us got out on deck in the morning. The scenery is a succession of well-wooded mountains, down whose sides, like long white ribbons, trickled the silver threads of waterfalls fed by the eternal snows which crown their tops Numerous islands dotted the straits and bays through which we passed. All were well wooded, and will supply lumber and timber for the markets for years to come. Frequently on the mountain sides, reaching far toward the snow-line, were seen narrow strips of different shades of green. These, we were told, marked the tracks of avalanches, which, in rushing down the mountains, had carried everything before them, and a new growth had sprung up, accounting for the difference in color of the foliage. Here in these mountains is the home of the bald eagle, the emblem of our nation. At all times of the day some of these noble birds were seen either soaring over the steamer or perched upon the highest limbs of the tallest trees that grow near the water. An officer of the boat informed me that at some seasons of the year hundreds of them could be seen in a single day.

Bulletins were posted in the social hall and smoking-room at noon of each day, giving the number of miles traveled the preceding twenty-four hours, the straits, bays and sounds through which we were to pass, and the time when the vessel was expected to reach certain points. These were eagerly scanned as soon as posted, and many of the passengers made copies of every bulletin.

There were quite a number of fine musicians on board, and every evening a number of them would take possession of social hall and give an entertainment, which added much to the pleasure of the trip. Among the party were a couple of sisters who were expert musicians, one performing on the mandolin and the other accompanying her on the piano. They were always in demand, and no entertainment was thought of unless they were in it. The young ladies were Hebrews, ac-companied by their father and mother, and they appreciated every attention that was shown them.

After leaving Victoria everybody was on the lookout for a whale, and numerous false alarms were sounded by those who, anxious to be the first to see one of these monsters of the deep, let their imaginations get the better of them. To some persons porpoises appeared as whales ; to others floating logs, and so on. A small reef just above water was mistaken for a whale by a young lady, and she never heard the last of it until the boat landed at Victoria on its return. One afternoon, however, a number were sighted and there was a rush for the bow of the boat to see them. There must have been at least two dozen, and they spouted at frequent intervals. We watched them until they disappeared far in the wake of the steamer.

On the afternoon of the third day from Tacoma we met the steamer "Islander," with a number of excursionists returning from Alaska. The vessels were made fast to each other. Those on the "Islander" were anxious to hear the latest news from the national convention at Minneapolis, and were glad to take what papers we had, even though a week old. After visiting each other for about half an hour the vessels parted company, the "Queen" continuing to the north and the "Islander" to the south. It was a pleasing and novel experience, and was appreciated by all.

After leaving the northern boundary of Washington we had sailed for almost two days in British waters, but when we commenced crossing Dixon Entrance the captain informed us that we were sailing within the territory of the United States — Alaska.

The first settlement noticed was that of Metla-kathla, an Indian town founded by a missionary named Duncan. It is self-supporting and under no particular church, but the founder is of the old Scotch Presbyterian faith.

One evening while promenading the deck our attention was drawn to notes of music from the violin and banjo. Following the direction of the sounds we came upon a number of the waiters and room-boys engaged in shelling peas. Four young men seated upon a coil of rope were playing lively tunes on the violin, flute, banjo and accordion. A number of passengers, including several ladies, had been attracted to the same place and were engaged in helping the boys. It was a pleasant diversion and was enjoyed by all who participated in it.

Our first landing in Alaska was at Fort Wran-gle, an old Russian settlement. During the occupation of the territory by that nation it was a place of considerable importance and a garrison was kept there. Since the United States secured possession the soldiers have been withdrawn and the fort is fast going to decay. The town is a miserable looking place, with only one street, along which are numerous Indian shanties.

Long before the "Queen" had been made fast to the wharf and the gang-plank put ashore, the Indians were seen coming with their baskets and trinkets to sell to the tourists at exorbitant prices. They were dressed or wrapped in their many-colored blankets, and looked very picturesque. The baskets were very pretty and the trinkets consisted of wooden forks and spoons, with grotesque figures of heads, fish and turtles for handles. They also had small totem-poles, with such figures carved on them as only an Alaskan Indian could imagine. Fort Wrangle bears the distinction of having the finest totem-poles in the territory bordering on the ocean. They were easily seen, long before the steamer came to the wharf, lifting their grotesque figures in front of the Indian shanties that face the bay. The totems are varieties of ancestral crests, marking the different families of which the household consists. Some of the houses have two poles in front, representing both sides of the family. The heads of the families claim to trace their origin from either the crow, the whale, the wolf, the bear or the eagle. When the families intermarry, the different animals or birds and a number of

Totem-Poles, Fort Wrangle.

grotesque faces are carved on the immense poles, which are placed in front of the dwellings. Some of the graves are marked by curious blocks of wood, representing the whale, the wolf, etc.

> "And they painted on the grave posts
> Of the graves yet unforgotten,
> Each his own ancestral totem,
> Each the symbol of his household—
> Figure of the bear and reindeer,
> Of the turtle, crane and beaver."

The totem is held in great veneration by the families, and it is an unpardonable sin to sell or part with it.

While the steamer lay at the wharf an opportunity was given to those who wished to see a representation of the ancient war-dance given by an old Indian. We were all crowded into a large building, the same being black with smoke and reeking with numerous bad odors, which were somewhat purified by the smoking embers of a fire which struggled hard for existence in the centre of the room. After a long wait the Indian appeared, dressed in a *robe de nuit* and a pair of white muslin drawers, with a curiously marked blanket thrown over his shoulders. A peculiar-looking crown, open at the top and filled with the down of the sea-gull, adorned his ugly, painted head. He was preceded by an Indian beating furiously on a tom-tom and giving ear-splitting yells. Coming into the building, he explained the kind of a dance he was about to execute, when, at a given signal, the tom-toms were beaten and a chorus of Indian maidens set up a curious yell, and then the performer commenced to jump around, yelling and beating two sticks which he held in his hands. Throwing his head back with a quick jerk he sent the feathers flying from his head-dress all over the audience, who beat a hasty retreat and spent the rest of their time in picking the feathers off their clothes. In relating our experience to one of the citizens of the place he informed us that we had been "raked in," and that this Indian was one of the worst reprobates in the place. He said that the people would rather pay fifty cents each to have some one shoot him than to pay that amount to see him perform.

Drawn up on the beach in front of the huts were many canoes belonging to the Indians. Some of them were works of experts and showed evidences of great skill on the part of the makers. They are made from the yellow cedar, which is found in some parts of Alaska, where it attains a large growth. Those we saw on the beach were covered with boughs or old blankets, to prevent the sun from warping or cracking the sides. The utmost care is taken of them, as the canoe is the Indian's chief means of earning a livelihood. In times when they were engaged in war with neighboring tribes, canoes that carried from thirty to fifty people were in use. The largest one seen upon the beach was probably forty feet in length. An Indian without a canoe is in a pitiable plight.

The Alaskan women are not unlike their more civilized sisters in one respect—the love of display of jewelry. Many of them were adorned with numerous rings and bracelets, which they would sell to the tourists at good prices. A peculiar adornment was the labrette worn by them in their lower lip. The lip is pierced and a small piece of silver inserted, and as this "ornament" is something out of the ordinary style of the more enlightened nations, one of our party bought one from a wrinkled old squaw who was selling garnets. Some of the younger girls had their faces painted black, believing it added to their beauty.

As we walked along the only street of the village and stopped to purchase some trinkets exhibited for sale, the mixture of unwholesome odors that came from the dwellings was nauseous, and it was a great relief to get back to the steamer and breathe the pure air as it came from the bay uncontaminated by contact with the natives.

Halibut Hook.

Among our purchases was a peculiar-looking fish hook, used for catching halibut. It is gro·tesquely carved, like all things used by the Alaskans.

It was after midnight when the lines were cast off and we were again steaming northward. In the morning we were very much surprised to see that the steamer was not moving and that numerous icebergs were floating quite near. Directly in front of the vessel was an immense wall of ice, surmounted by innumerable glistening pinnacles. It was a beautiful sight. The coloring of the glacier, for such it was, surpassed anything we had ever seen. The pinnacles were a snowy white, while the ice below varied from a delicate green to an ultramarine blue. We were at the Taku glacier, where the supply of ice for the round trip was taken on board. Large cakes of ice were brought up to the ship, a strong wire net thrown around them, and then they were hoisted on board. It was an interesting sight to watch the work, and after forty tons had been stored in the hold the vessel was turned about and we proceeded to Douglass Island, our next stopping-place. Here are located the famous Treadwell gold mines, the largest in the world. An opportunity was given the passengers to visit these mines, and most of them embraced it. We first went into the stamp mill, but hastily withdrew on account of the noise, which was almost deafening. A number of

Taking on Ice, Taku Bay.

the ladies were presented with some very fine specimens of pyrites, or "fools' gold," which they at first thought were very valuable. Back of the stamp-mill is the mine. It resembles a quarry more than anything else, as the rock is all above ground. From here we passed to the roasting room, where large furnaces heated the pulverized stone and released what gold remained after the washing in the stamp-mill. The mine is a mountain of ore. It was discovered by a man named Treadwell (after whom it was named), who sold it to four men for $500. They expended a sufficient amount of money to demonstrate the value of the mine, and sold it to a stock company, each man receiving $750,000 in cash, besides a considerable amount of stock. The mine is now valued at $25,000,000. The ore is what is termed "low-grade," and averages between five and eight dollars from each ton of rock. The cost of reducing the ore varies from one dollar to one dollar and ninety cents per ton, so one can see that it is a bonanza of the largest kind.

After spending over an hour looking through the works and surroundings, we went back to the steamer. Soon the lines were cast off, and we steamed for Juneau, just across the bay.

Juneau is a picturesque little town nestled at
the base of a high mountain. It is a place of
some importance, but as we approached it did
not seem very inviting. It is a fitting-out place
for prospectors, who make up their packs here
and go over the mountains in search of gold.
Here our miners left the boat and began looking
around for Indians to carry their packs. One of
them had a most striking physique—large,
powerful and well-proportioned. In conversation with him it was ascertained that he was
going to work his way over the mountains until
he got to the Yukon river, then prospect along
its banks until he reached the Behring sea,
where he would probably get on an American
war vessel and come back to civilization. He
calculated that he would be gone all summer,
and would get back to the States about the
middle of November. The passengers bought.
numerous baskets and trinkets, for which they
paid, as usual, extravagant prices. On board
the vessel were many delegates to the Presbyterian Assembly, which met at Portland, Oregon,
and a reception was tendered them by the Presbyterian inhabitants of the town. It was given
in the little opera house and was a very pleasant
affair. We were all satisfied to leave when the

time came, as the weather had been very thick and rainy.

As we steamed farther north great numbers of cormorants were seen. They belong to the pelican family, and are notorious because of their gluttonous habits. Their food is principally fish, and they eat such quantities that their wings are unable to lift them out of the water, and consequently they are not able to fly. It was very amusing to watch their efforts to get out of the way of the vessel, and to see them floundering over the water. Sometimes they would turn completely over.

Our next landing-place was Sitka, the capital of the territory, but before touching there we went to Chilkat, the northernmost point reached on our trip. It was early in the morning, and not over a dozen people were on deck when the steamer, passing Chilkat, turned her prow to the south and started for Sitka. Before reaching our destination we passed through Peril straits, the most dangerous part of the trip. It seemed to most of the passengers as if nothing could prevent the vessel from being wrecked upon the many rocks, but the stanch craft was skillfully guided past them and gracefully outrode all danger.

We arrived in Sitka Saturday evening, just after dinner, and the customary array of Indian squaws was seen squatting along the wharf, with their trinkets spread out before them. The usual high prices prevailed, and the tourists soon returned to the boat with armloads of totem-

Baronoff Castle, Sitka.

sticks, small canoes, baskets, canoe-paddles, and other things too numerous to mention. The first building worthy of attention was the old Baronoff castle. It stands upon a rock near the wharf. It was the residence of the Russian governors before Alaska was acquired by the United States. During the residency of the Romanoff governors its halls witnessed many brilliant gatherings when the naval commanders and envoys visited the territory. It is said that the wife of the ruling governor, when the terri-tory was ceded to the United States, shed many bitter tears when the Russian flag was lowered and the Stars and Stripes run up in its place. She was far more patriotic than the officials, and looked upon the selling of the domain as an indication of waning power. The castle is now unoccupied and fast approaching destruction. From the cupola on the roof a fine view of the town and bay may be had. The village is built at the base of a range of mountains whose crests are continually covered with snow. The street follows the contour of the bay, is perhaps a mile or more in length, and reaches from the "rancherie" to the Indian river. Turning, one looks upon a most beautiful harbor and bay, studded with numerous islands.

At anchor in the bay were several United States war vessels with the seal-poachers they had captured while illegally catching seals on the islands.

Directly in front of the wharf, some distance

Main Street and Greek Church, Sitka.

from the water, is the only Greek church in America. It is built in the form of a cross, surmounted by a steeple that was once painted green, but which is now badly faded. A Maltese cross crowns the spire. As services were not being held, an admission fee of fifty cents was charged. The interior was magnificently furnished with paintings by the old masters. In the pictures of the saints and the Madonna only the faces are seen, the balance being covered with gold or silver. The crowns worn by brides and bridegrooms at marriage ceremonies were shown us; also the bishop's miter. The latter was very old, and, being set with pearls and precious stones, was very valuable. Several entertaining hours could easily have been spent within the sacred walls, but as our time was limited we hurried through.

The Indians are kept as much as possible in a section of the town called the "rancherie." In visiting it one finds a bottle of smelling-salts very acceptable, as the odors which issue from the cabins are oppressive. It was after eleven o'clock, Saturday evening, when the writer passed through it hunting for Princess Thom, a fat, wrinkled Indian squaw who has amassed a small fortune in trading among her tribe and

with the white people. It was a surprise to
realize, on arriving at the boat, that though
almost midnight, darkness had not yet settled
down, owing to the long twilight, and several
on deck were yet engaged in reading at this
hour.

Sunday morning was bright and clear. Before
breakfast a party of us started out to revisit the
"rancherie" and get some silver spoons, made
by the natives. Noticing a great number of
mongrel curs in this part of the town, our curiosity was aroused and we counted as many as a
dozen in front of several of the huts. The average to each cabin was about nine. After securing what trinkets we wanted we returned to the
steamer, meeting on the way a number of our
fellow-passengers bent on the same errand as our
own. We strolled through the old cemetery and
noticed quite a number of small houses about the
size of dog-kennels over many of the graves.
Some were provided with windows and others
were enclosed on all sides. On the way back we
noticed several octagonal buildings, which, during the Russian occupation, had been used as
magazines and block-houses. They have long
since been abandoned and are fast going to
decay.

Flying around the warehouses and buildings near the wharf were numerous large ravens, fully twice the size of the crows of our native clime. They gave a much louder "caw" than their more southern brethren and seemed to jeer at us as we passed them. In former times, before the Christianizing of the natives, many of the tribes of Alaska held this bird sacred, some families tracing their origin back to it.

Some of the tourists spent the day visiting the missions, while others took a walk along the romantic Indian river, which flows immediately in the rear of the town. We chose the latter, and wended our way through the grounds be-longing to the mission, back past the cemetery, through numerous patches of wild flowers, where we found the path leading to the river. It was a romantic walk through forests of pine and over rustic bridges, with the clear waters of the Indian river running at our side. Several hours were spent as we sauntered along, and by the time we arrived at the wharf it was almost time for us to start for Muir Glacier.

Before the vessel left the wharf a number of us bought copies of the only newspaper pub-lished in the city. It was made up of "patent outsides" of several varieties, giving descrip

tions of various points of interest in the territory.
The "news" was on the inside, and was made
up principally of a list of passengers of the
steamer.   An Indian band from the Presbyterian
mission came down to the wharf and played
several airs, and Princess Thom, wrapped in one
of her finest blankets, came to bid us adieu.

Mount Edgecombe, whose summit pierces the
clouds, is an extinct volcano located on the
southern point of Kruzoff Island, opposite the
city of Sitka.   Its elevation is 2,955 feet, and
the crater is 2,000 feet across and 400 feet deep.
It is the sacred mount of the Alaskan Indians.
What Olympus was to the ancient Greeks, Edgecombe is to the uncivilized tribes of Alaska.   I
will repeat, as near as I can, one of the tradi-
tions related to me as a party of us sat on the
upper deck of the steamer upon leaving the
wharf :

"In the dim and distant past," according to
the Indian legend, "the first Indian pair lived
under the shadow of this mountain.   For a long
time they lived happily together, and many children were the fruit of their marriage.   One day,
like a thunder-clap out of a clear sky, a family
jar occurred, and the husband and wife quarreled
long and loud.   The Great Spirit, as a punish-

ment for their unseemly conduct, changed the man into a wolf and the woman into a raven. The latter then flew to the crater of the mount and disappeared within it, and is now supposed to be resting upon a stump, supporting the world upon her outstretched wings. Whenever there is a storm. accompanied with thunder and lightning, the natives believe that it is only the ravings of the wolf who is trying to dislodge the raven from her resting-place, and should he succeed the world and all upon it will be destroyed."

And now, even with all the influences of Christianity thrown about them, whenever it thunders many of the Indians take stones and pound upon the floors of their houses to encourage the raven to hold fast to her resting place.

At twelve o'clock Sunday noon the steamer glided gracefully through the channels between the many islands that dot the harbor in front of Sitka. Passing through Peril straits, we were again moving toward the north. It was a little after ten o'clock when the first iceberg was sighted—a small one, about the size of an ordinary one-story frame cottage. It was not long before they commenced to get quite numerous, and before two o'clock in the morning, when we

retired, they were scraping the paint off the iron
hull of our vessel.

On awaking Monday morning the prospects of
a clear day seemed doubtful, but before breakfast

Ice-Floe, Glacier Bay.

was over the rays of the sun had pierced the
clouds, and everyone was in a happy mood.
The "Queen" lay within two miles of the great
Muir Glacier, although it looked much nearer.

There it was, an immense mountain of ice, moving forward at the rate of about forty feet per day. It looked as if the immense waves of an angry ocean had suddenly become frozen and were waiting for the warm rays of the sun to restore them to life again. At intervals immense pieces would break off and fall into the water, accompanied with a rumbling noise like that of distant thunder. The glacier extends from shore to shore, a distance of four miles, and lifts its pinnacles four hundred feet above the muddy river. It was my fortune to see one of the tallest of these break off and plunge into the river. When it struck, the spray was thrown far above the highest point of the glacier. The roar that accompanied the fall was terrific.

Those who wished to climb the glacier, after providing themselves with alpenstocks, were rowed ashore. It is not dangerous to climb, providing one exercises ordinary prudence and does not attempt venturesome explorations on his own account. A hard climb of about three miles, which seemed more like ten, over the moraine, brought us to the glacier proper. After climbing several of the ridges we started on our return trip in order to get lunch before coming out in the afternoon. Those three miles seemed

Landing at Muir Glacier.

to lengthen at every step, and we were surely a tired and hungry party when we arrived on board the steamer. On our return we plucked a bouquet of beautiful purple flowers which were blooming not ten feet from the snow and ice that formed the mighty glacier. A good lunch was provided, and after a short rest we determined to walk to the foot of the glacier by way of the beach. The whole afternoon was spent on the sands, where the sun was piping hot, blistering our faces and ears equal to an August day at the seaside in far-away New Jersey. A photographer conveniently happened along, and we induced him to photograph our party as we sat perched upon a stranded iceberg.

All afternoon there was a constant roar, caused by falling pinnacles and the parting of the glacier. Most of the noise came from the interior, as very few pieces fell from the front during the entire day. Pieces breaking off underneath the glacier would be carried some distance by the swift current before coming to the surface, and if very large they would cause immense waves to roll upon the shore. Captain Carroll said that in all his experience of nine years he had not seen so few pieces fall.

Returning to the steamer we found several

Muir Glacier.

canoes, each one containing two Indians who had for sale the usual stock of trinkets, consisting of baskets, small canoes, paddles, bone and ivory images and horn and wooden spoons. They belonged to the Chilkoot tribe of Indians and had come over one hundred miles to sell their trinkets. Even after they had disposed of considerable of their stock and were unable to make any more bargains they were loth to leave, but remained near the steamer until the wheels of the propeller began churning the water, when they gave a series of grunts and paddled off toward home to replenish their stock and be back for the next steamer in about a week.

At seven o'clock the anchor was hoisted and the noble "Queen" steamed quite near the glacier, where the captain blew the whistle several times, the echo of which reverberated through the pinnacles and valleys of the glacier again and again. Just as we were leaving an immense fall of ice occurred, giving us a parting salute as if trying to make up for its inaction during the day.

Alaska, being a comparatively new country, abounds in legends. Among the most wonderful is the one freely told that under the muddy

14

waters of the Glacier river a submerged city is
to be seen.   Through its centre runs a river
along which are wharves where ships lie at
anchor.   An ivy-mantled church and the grave-
yard adjoining are all said to be seen under
favorable conditions.   These conditions were not
apparent while the steamer "Queen" lay at
anchor on June 13th, 1892, two miles from the
glacier.   A few of the passengers, we afterwards
ascertained, looked wistfully over the sides of the
steamer to secure a view of the silent city.
Mr. Willoughby, after whom Wiloughby's
island was named, claims to have seen the city
faithfully reflected in the sky above the river,
but he evidently saw a mirage, as the river is
too muddy to reflect anything six inches below
the surface.

After we had steamed out of Glacier bay, with
its floating icebergs, the utmost quiet seemed to
prevail.   Everybody had retired, tired out with
the many absorbing sights of the day, reminding
one of the weariness which comes over children
on Christmas night, after the excitements of the
day have worn them into a condition for seeking
their beds.   Our party had been in a constant
state of excitement previous to seeing the glacier,
but now that they had seen it and had climbed

over it they were willing to take a much-needed rest and make up some of the lost sleep of the nights before.

The return trip was without incident, save a little episode while crossing Millbank Sound, when a number of passengers, on account of the rolling of the vessel, paid their respects to old Neptune. Here we witnessed for the first time the phenomena of phosphorescent sea. The wake of the vessel had the appearance of coals of fire, and we watched it for more than an hour.

One evening an entertainment was given by the young ladies and gentlemen of the party. The characters represented were mostly Alaskan, with the usual negro-minstrel attachment. Many of the articles bought by the tourists were brought out and put to some use. The affair was a success in every particular, and the audience contributed very liberally to the baskets as they were passed around. The money collected was donated to furnishing the parsonage of the Presbyterian missionary at Juneau.

One morning the steamer was noticed to slacken speed, and presently a small steamboat put out from the shore and made direct for us. In the bow were several Indians wrapped in their blankets. As the boat came alongside, a ladder was let down and a missionary (or "sky pilot," as one of the officers called him) climbed over the side and took his place among the Indians, who showed their love for him in many ways. He was going to one of the missionary stations and was to remain at his work for six months, during which time he did not expect to see the face of a white man. The Indians had brought out some fish and presented them to the captain, and we partook of fresh fish for the next two meals.

The only stop made on the return trip between Muir Glacier and Victoria was at the coaling-station near Nanaimo, where five hundred tons of coal were taken on board. While the purser was making arrangements for receiving the coal, the captain gave the passengers a pleasant surprise. The little steam-launch was hoisted from the hold and placed in the water ; then followed the boats from the davits, until seven of them were lying alongside the steamer. All who wished were then privileged to take their places in them, and we steamed off for the village of Nanaimo in tow of the steam launch. Two hours were allowed us to visit the places of interest. Nearly all went first to the jewelry stores and bought souvenir spoons, after which they looked about the town.

Nanaimo is one of the old Hudson Bay Trading Company's outposts, and the old bastion which once protected the white men from the Indians is still standing in one of the streets. The town owes much of its prosperity to the discovery of coal near it. The mines are an immense source of revenue to the proprietor, and the supply is apparently inexhaustible. They are owned by one Mr. Dunsmuir, whose castle in Victoria has been spoken of in the preceding pages.

Our return to the ship was as pleasant as the first sail, and we arrived there in time for a bountiful supper which had been prepared for us. Train after train of cars loaded with coal were being emptied of their contents into the hold. and there was ample time for those who wished to go on shore and hunt wild flowers.

The steamer remained at the wharf until the next morning, when it headed for Victoria. Here an hour was allowed to those who wished to revisit the city and make purchases. Quite a number of the passengers came near getting left. They were up town buying trinkets to take home, and the storekeepers informed them that they had plenty of time, as a street car passed the door every ten minutes for the wharf. They

waited fully twenty minutes for one to pass, and
had started to walk when it overtook them. It
poked along and managed to get within an
eighth of a mile of the wharf when the whistle
sounded that the lines were cast off. It was a
long run, but it had to be made, and the writer
was just able to jump and catch the anchor-
chains, when he climbed to the deck and informed the mate that there were several elderly
ladies on the way from the street car. The engines were then stopped and the gang plank put
out for them to come on board. It was a narrow
escape, and a situation which few would desire
in a country so foreign and remote.

At Seattle many of the passengers left the
steamer—some to take the train and others to
sojourn for a few weeks in that wonderful Western city. It was the breaking-up of our party
after the long trip from Philadelphia across the
continent, and from Mexico to Alaska, during
which time friendships were formed that will
live, it is to be hoped, for all time. Had it not
been for the stop at Nanaimo we should have
arrived at our starting place, Tacoma, one day
ahead of schedule time.

All were well pleased with the trip and with
the courtesies extended by Captain Carroll, who

did everything in his power to make the journey agreeable. No more careful captain sails the seas than he, and we commend his proud vessel, the "Queen," to all who make the journey to that wonderland of the Northwest—Alaska.

May his shadow never grow less.

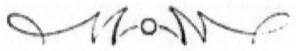

CHAPTER VI.

PORTLAND AND SHOSHONE.

IT WAS quite late in the evening when our
steamer was made fast to the wharf at Tacoma
and the passengers began to disembark. The
scene presented was a lively one. Some were
loaded with baskets filled with trinkets, others
were carrying large bundles and bags, while
many were followed by the ship's porters, who
were also loaded with bundles of every description. Each seemed bent on being the first to
get off the wharf. All had something to remind
them of the trip to Alaska. Some were hurrying
for the train, which stood waiting, and others
hustled themselves into omnibuses or cabs and
started for the hotel. We were among the latter.
Rooms being secured we were soon at home, as
this was our second visit to Tacoma.

Our stay was necessarily short, as we had
fully expected to be in Mount Carmel, Illinois,
the day we landed, had we not taken the trip
to Alaska. Having ordered our mail sent to
Portland we left early the next morning for the
latter place, arriving there in the evening. Here

we found a number of our fellow-passengers of the "Queen," who had come on the night before and were preparing to go to San Francisco and other points in California.

Portland is a beautiful city, situated on the Willamette river about twelve miles from its junction with the Columbia. It has nearly 65,000 inhabitants and is steadily forging ahead. Its business houses and residences compare favorably with any city in the West Having a letter of introduction to Mr. Cicero Lewis, I called on him at his palatial home, which, with the grounds surrounding it, occupies an entire block. While speaking of the wonderful growth of the city he remarked that when he first came to Portland he had killed deer on the ground upon which his house stood, and that only a few years ago it was a field of stumps. The city now extends miles beyond, and electric cars pass his door. The principal hotel in the city is named "The Portland," and is under the management of Mr. Charles E. Leland, one of that family of brothers so famous for their hotels.

From the hills of Portland can be distinctly seen the snow-capped peaks of Mt. Hood, Mt. St Helens and Mt. Ranier. At the wharves are to be seen ships of all nations discharging and receiving their cargoes.

Multnomah Falls.

Leaving Portland by the morning train, in order to obtain a view of the Columbia river, we entered upon what seemed to us the beginning of our homeward journey. The conductor, who was especially pleasant, exerted himself to show us points of interest which otherwise, in all likelihood, would have been passed unnoticed. At Multnomah Falls the train stopped several minutes to enable passengers to get out and view this beautiful fall. The cliff from which the falls leap is so high that the water becomes only a heavy cloud of mist before reaching the foot of the precipice. Several other interesting falls were passed, but, being much interested in the large fish-wheels, we had not opportunity to investigate them. The first wheel seen was on a boat, and appeared to be about twenty feet in diameter. It was continually revolving, being kept in motion by the force of the water. The largest wheels are to be seen at the Cascades, where they are supported by piers. They are kept continually going during the season in which the salmon run. The wheels are covered, except at the openings, with wire netting, and resemble large scoops. In revolving, they catch the fish that come within their reach and tumble them into a trough in the centre of the wheel,

Fish Wheel.

from which they fall out into the boat or a box and are taken to the canneries. The season was not fairly commenced when we passed, and the catches were consequently small.

As we were approaching the "Dalles," a tall shaft standing on an island was noticed. The island seemed bare of all vegetation, and would have passed unnoticed had it not been for the shaft. A passenger explained that it was a monument marking the grave of Victor Trevet, an eccentric old pioneer, who died some years ago. He was a great friend of the Indians and wished to be buried among them. The name of the island is Memaloose Isle, the interpretation of which means the "Isle of the Dead," and has been for many years the burial-place of the Chinook Indians.

Many are the legends associated with the points of interest along this beautiful river, and were it not for the space required in writing them we would gladly repeat some as they were told to us.

After leaving the "Dalles" a passenger pointed out an Indian village where the Indians have come, from time immemorial, and settled during the fishing season, speared their winter's supply of fish, and then returned to their hunting-

grounds in the mountains. Soon afterward the
railroad leaves the river and enters a country of
lava, rock and sand. The eyes soon become
weary of looking out of the car windows, and to
rest them the curtains are drawn and we try the
experiment of short naps for a change.

It was nearing noon of the second day out
from Portland when we arrived at Shoshone, a
small town of less than a thousand inhabitants,
located in the lava-beds of southern Idaho. It
owes its existence to the fact that here is the
junction of a branch of the Union Pacific railroad leading up to the mining camps of the
Wood river, and that it is the nearest point to
the Great Shoshone Falls of the Snake river.
Most of the houses are built of dark lava-blocks,
which gives the town an ancient but substantial
appearance. Along the main street and around
the homes of the wealthier members of the community are cottonwood shade-trees. Irrigating
ditches supply moisture for their roots, and they
flourish. There are two hotels for the accommodation of tourists *en route* for the falls. Having
made our arrangements for a stage to convey us
to the falls, considerable delay was experienced on account of a drunken blacksmith
who was engaged to shoe two of the horses,

and it was three o'clock when we got into
t'e old rattle-trap stage and started for a
ride of twenty five miles across the lava-beds.
Our driver, who was one of the proprietors of the stage line, had only been married a
week, and his wife, a very handsome young lady,
occupied the box, sitting between her husband
and the writer. When everything was ready,
and good-byes had been exchanged, the driver
cracked his whip and off the four horses started
at a gallop. We were soon out of sight of the
village, and were in the lava-beds. On either
side, as far as the eye could reach, was nothing
but sage-brush and cactus-plants. Near the road
great quantities of yellow and white flowers gave
relief to the eye, and occasionally the brilliant
red or the rich amber-colored flowers of the cactus were to be seen. There was a gentle breeze
stirring, which made the ride very pleasant, and
also carried away the dust. As we drove along,
the young lady and bride entered into the general conversation, and proved herself a very
interesting adjunct to our party during this novel
ride.

After we had driven about three hours we
inquired where the falls were, and if they could
be seen, as the landscape still presented nothing

but sage-brush, lava, flowers and parched grass. We were told to wait a while and we would see them before we expected. As we proceeded we entered what appeared to be a natural gate, and commenced a descent of over one thousand feet to the bottom of Snake river cañon, in which are the falls. In making one of the sharp turns in the road the first view of the falls was had. Here we had to get out and walk down, as the road is so steep that it is dangerous to ride. At the ferry, only two-hundred yards above the falls, the river is said to be over two hundred feet deep, and the rushing of the muddy water made the more timid ones of the party wish that the hotel could be reached without crossing it. Our driver assured them that there was no danger, as there were two heavy wire cables reaching from shore to shore, one under the water, to which was attached the windlass for propelling the boat, and a safety cable above the water, over which a trolley worked as the boat moved. We were soon over, and driving up to the cosy hotel found ourselves the only guests, and were accorded the freedom of the house.

The hotel is built quite near the falls, and from the porch a fine view of the second Niagara is to be had. The wind, blowing in the direction of the hotel, carried spray in such quantities that it appeared as if a heavy rain were falling. The force of the falling water jarred the hotel continually, and it was some time before we could accustom ourselves to it. Above the falls are several islands. On one of them an eagle has built her nest, and there, amid the ceaseless roar of the falling water, has reared her young for years. She is safe from the depredations of man, as no human being has ever been able to reach the rock.

The width of the falls proper is 950 feet, and of the Bridal Veil 125 feet. The first rush of the water is a fall of over eighty feet, but the final plunge is over a precipice 210 feet into a seething and boiling stream. In the morning when the sun rose over the surrounding cliffs and penetrated the clouds of mist that rose from the boiling caldron below the falls, beautiful rainbows were formed in quick succession as the clouds of spray were blown hither and yon by the winds.

It is not known when the Shoshone Falls were discovered, as no mention of them is made by the emigrants who must have passed quite near them on their way to the Pacific during the stirring times of the gold excitement in 1849.

Shoshone Falls.

But, like all other places, it has its legends.   It is said that in the sands of Bell's Island, just at the brink of the falls, gold is to be found; and where gold is, men will go.   From our driver we learned that a miner named Tom Bell had a claim upon the island which now bears his name. It was his custom to remain on the island until his provisions got low, when he would come to the mainland to replenish his stock.   One day when returning to the mainland one of his oars snapped while he was in the rapids, and the sequel was that poor Tom went over the falls and his body was never recovered.   Several China-men, it is reported, have shared the fate of Bell, but as a Chinaman's life is not considered worth counting in this country, there is no clear record as to how many Celestials have taken the leap.

The best view of the falls is obtained at Obser-vation Point, directly in front of the hotel.   A narrow path leads out to it.   Pushing one's way through the juniper bushes, one feels the damp spray falling upon him like rain.   A wire cable stretched along the edge of the cliff forms a guard for those who wish to get the view from this point.   The rushing of the waters causes a strong current of air, and one must hold to the cable lest he be blown into the waters at the foot

of the falls. The view from this point is grand.
The waters above the falls, broken by the
rapids, are churned to a milky whiteness, and
dash against the rocky islands as if to hurl
them from their foundations. Defeated in
their work, they rush forward, apparently mad-
dened by their unsuccessful attempt, and with a
terrible roar plunge over the precipice into the
boiling caldron 210 feet below. The waters be
low the falls, still fretful but crowned with masses
of white foam, press onward through the cañon
until, disappearing around one of the curves in
the river, they are lost sight of and the black
walls of the cañon arrest one's view.

Below the falls are the Natural Bridge and
Diana's Bath-Room. The latter is a large grotto,
in the centre of which is a natural basin into
which drop the waters from the roof of the cave.
There are several other caves, and in one the
rushing of the waters suggests the passage of
a large steamer, and one can hear the repeated
strokes of the paddle wheels as they strike the
water. To reach the bottom of the falls and
return is no small job, as it is one continual
climb excepting when at the water's edge.

Three miles up the cañon are the Twin Falls.
An island in mid-stream divides the river into

two channels, each about seventy feet in width, through which the waters rush. At the lower end of the island the river takes a plunge of one hundred and eighty feet into a circular basin, resembling a boiling and seething caldron, from which rise dense clouds of spray.

While waiting for Mr. Walgamot to bring his ferry-boat so that we could re-cross the river, one of the party who had heard that sage bush tea was a sure preventive of baldheadedness employed considerable time in gathering an immense handful of it to apply to his already shining pate. I have met him several times since my return from the West, and his cranium has lost none of its polish, nor has the skating-rink on the top of his head diminished in size.

Walking up the roadway leading to the mesa we had an opportunity to notice the column-like prisms which the lava, in cooling, had formed. It was quite a climb, and we were thankful that we had left our wraps in the stage upon leaving the ferry-boat. Before reaching the top of the cañon we took a last look at Shoshone Falls and left them in their lonely grandeur.

Taking our seats in the stage we returned at a lively rate to Shoshone. A gentle breeze was stirring, and upon the advice of Mr. Perrine we put our wraps about us. Before reaching the town we were glad that we had followed his suggestion.

It was noon when we arrived in Shoshone, and the time between that and the departure of the train was spent in looking over the town. While in one of the stores several Indians came in and wanted to trade some gloves made from buckskin. They were Shoshones and were well formed, as straight as arrows, and, wrapped in their blankets, made a novel and interesting appearance. When the train pulled into the station, we were on the platform ready to start for new scenes.

Chapter VII.

WONDERLAND.

Leaving Shoshone our faces were once more turned to the east. The scenery along the way was nothing to boast of, especially after leaving the Columbia river, and we soon became tired looking out of the car windows and turned our attention to reading such papers as we could purchase from the newsboy on the train. Occasionally we would pass a neat farm or ranch which would seem a veritable oasis in the desert. The water used for irrigating these ranches is sometimes brought for miles in ditches or pipes, and wherever used the desert blossoms like the rose.

Frequently we would see, in the distance, buttes or hills that arose abruptly from the desert. Some seemed about two hundred feet high, but many of them were evidently much higher. They were bare of vegetation, excepting now and then a clump of grease-weed, and had a forbidding appearance. The country being bare of trees, we had an uninterrupted view for miles on either side. One afternoon, while on one of the plateaus, we noticed far down in the valley what appeared to be a town of some importance. Between us and the town was a railroad train, moving at what seemed to us about at right angles to the course we were taking. Watching it for some time we discovered that it would soon pass us, as it was a train bound in the opposite direction upon the same railroad.

At the American Falls of the Snake river the train halted for a few moments upon the bridge, the piers of which were built in the midst of the rushing torrent. From here on to Pocatella was the same scenery—sand and lava.

It was near five o'clock when we arrived at Pocatella, where we changed cars and took the Utah Northern branch of the Union Pacific railroad. While waiting for our train we noticed quite a number of Indians, wrapped in their blankets, walking around the station. They were tall, well formed, and as straight as arrows. One in particular attracted much attention. His face was painted in several colors, giving him a grotesque appearance. In his hair were at least half a dozen eagle feathers, and around his body was wrapped a many-colored blanket. His leggins were ornamented with several rows of brightly-polished steel keys, which, as he moved, would strike together, making a tinkling sound. These Indians were strikingly different from those we saw in Alaska. When we pulled out of the station several of them got on the platforms of the cars and rode as far as they wished and then dropped off. The Indians never pay any car-fare, but usually ride on freight trains or on the platforms of the passenger cars. They are not allowed inside unless in extremely cold weather.

Just outside of the limits of Pocatella is an Indian reservation, which accounted for the number of red men seen in and around the station. Some of the Indians live in log houses built for them by the government, but most of them prefer the wigwams, many of which were scattered along the road for some distance.

At Idaho Falls we again crossed the Snake river. These falls are not so precipitous as the American Falls, and resemble only a series of rapids. Here quite a number of the passengers got off, as it was near sheep shearing time, and the owners of the large ranches had been down the road engaging men for clipping the sheep.

It was after dark when the train pulled into the station at Beaver Cañon, where we were to stop over night and take the stages in the morning for the Yellowstone National Park, or "Wonderland," as it is most appropriately christened by men who have traveled the world over. As it was late we were unable to procure a warm supper, as the proprietor of the only hotel in the place had not been advised of our coming, and we feasted upon bread and cheese sandwiches. In the morning a steaming hot breakfast awaited us. It was not brought on in courses, but everything was well cooked and neatly served. The proprietor was a Dane and did many favors for us, including the taking care of our trunks, which we were unable to take with us into the park. He had been quite a traveler, and during his life had prospected for gold.

Before the stage drove up to the door we were advised to procure some mosquito-netting for veils, as the mosquitoes were likely to bother us in some localities. Just as we were about starting we were joined by a young man who had come down from Butte, and was going into the Park. He was a Yankee, and afforded us considerable amusement. He pretended to be quite a marksman, but his pretentions came to naught. We had scarcely passed over the brow of the first hill after leaving the cañon when we were startled by the firing of a pistol in the front of the coach. It was our Yankee fellow-traveler shooting at a woodchuck, which escaped unharmed.

The country through which we were passing was like an immense flower-garden. For miles on either side, as far as the eye could reach, flowers were in profusion. The prevailing colors were white, yellow, blue, and occasionally a pink or red flower was noticed. So interwoven were they that the whole country had the appearance of an immense carpet spread out over the hills and valley.

Here our mosquito-netting came into use. The pestiferous things rose in clouds from every ford or marshy place we crossed. They made life almost a burden. We fought them with our hands and bathed our necks and wrists in menthol to keep them away, but to no purpose. They were after us and were going to stay with us. In the dining-room at the dinner-station on the Camas Meadows the window panes were black with them and we were compelled to eat with our veils on, but that did not prevent them from getting into our mouths. For two long hours we were at their mercy—hard, unrelenting, unmerciful mercy. They bit us until our necks,

faces and hands had the appearance of being
stung by a swarm of bees. Outside of the cabin
they were even worse, and appeared in clouds
whenever the grass was stirred. We had to
keep moving, for the instant we stopped they
would light upon our clothes so thick that we
could not tell the color of the cloth. After one
blow upon the shoulder of our Yankee friend,
thirty-four dead mosquitoes were found sticking
to his coat. We were all thankful when the
driver told us to take our places in the stage
for our departure.

Numerous curlews, with their long curled bills,
were to be seen upon all sides, and our Yankee
friend was busily employed trying to bag one.
At first we were somewhat afraid he might, but
we soon ceased to be alarmed for their safety and
became more worried for the life of the driver,
who was the nearest to our amateur marksman.
During the whole day he only bagged one little
bird, and that was not hit, but killed by concus-
sion.

Houses were few and far between, as lands
were taken principally by large companies and
devoted to stock-raising. At one ranch, near the
scene of a bloody battle between General How-
ard and the Indians, were a number of elk which

had been captured during the past winter, after a severe snow-storm. They were in a corral, and appeared quite tame. There were about twenty of them, and the driver drew up rein that we might have a better view of the handsome creatures.

Arangee Ranch, or Snake river crossing, was our stopping-place for the night. It is a collection of log cabins, none of which are over one story in height. It is the headquarters of several ranches owned by a company of New York capitalists engaged in stock-raising. Most of the cabins are occupied by the hands employed by this colony. Only one building is set apart for the accommodation of tourists. The situation of the cabins is beautiful. In the background are the heavy forests of pine, while in front is the swift running Snake river, beyond which lie the prairie, the foothills and the snow-capped mountains.

The sun was just dipping behind the mountains when we forded the river and drove up to the cabins. It was a most beautiful sight to look upon the snow-capped peaks, above which were the variously tinted clouds through which shot the brilliant rays of the setting sun. It was a picture to be seen only in these Western skies,

Arrangee Ranch.

and one that could never be transferred to canvas.

The mosquitoes were plentiful, but were not so numerous as they had been during the day. On being assigned our rooms we took the precaution to kill every one that could be found, thereby no doubt saving ourselves much affliction during the night.

Leaving Arangee Ranch early in the morning, we commenced a day of many surprises. At several places quite a number of deer, elk and antelope were seen.

About the middle of the forenoon we forded the Snake river for the last time until we should return from "Wonderland." The water of this river is said to be the coldest in the world, as it comes from the melting snows which crown the peaks forming the southern boundary of the Yellowstone National Park. In order to avoid several dangerous holes we made quite a detour, first going up stream and then down, finally emerging from the river almost opposite the place of entrance.

Most of the time we rode in sight of the Tetons, at whose base the wandering Snake river has its source. As we were crossing the "continental divide" in the Tyghee Pass and entering Montana, the axle of the stage became hot

Fording the Snake River.

and we spent almost an hour trying to cool it off with snow, which we procured from a ten-foot drift along the roadside. It was nearly noon when the accident occurred, and as some of the party had brought luncheon with them we en-joyed a picnic in a grove over ten thousand feet above sea-level.

It was about three o'clock when the stage pulled up at a very pretentious two-story log house, and the driver informed us that this was where we would stop over night. No one com-ing to the door, we walked in and took posses-sion. The reception room was large and airy ; in fact, it took up one half of the house and reached from the first floor to the roof. In one end of it were quite a number of bear skins, and hang-ing on the walls were skins of the otter, mink and various other animals. The bed-rooms were six in number and opened out-upon the recep-tion-room. Three were on the first floor and three above them, arranged like cells in a prison. Those on the second tier were reached by a flight of steps and along a balcony. The rooms were all newly furnished and neatly kept.

The proprietor, Mr. Dwelle, was a bachelor, and was the only person around the place. When he saw us coming he started off to catch a mess

of trout for supper.   Our Yankee friend and my-
self, after procuring some fishing-lines, followed
him.   In crossing a brook the writer made a misstep and fell into the water, which necessitated
his returning to the house to dry his clothes.
While sitting in front of the stove he was startled
by a crash, and looking out of the window saw
the back porch in ruins.   The ladies, who had
retired to their sleeping apartments for a rest,
appeared almost immediately in the wildest state
of excitement, anxiously inquiring if a cyclone
had struck the house.   Their fears being quieted
they returned to finish their naps.   Upon going
into the yard we ascertained that a number
of horses in prancing around had run against a
rope stretched from one of the out-buildings to
one of the supports of the porch, and, pulling
the latter from its place, the whole structure came
down with a crash.   It was not long before our
Yankee friend was seen returning.   He had met
with a similar mishap as the writer, only that he
had fallen in much deeper water, and did not have
a dry thread on him.   He went to a hunter's camp,
and having built a large fire, dried his clothing.
By damming one of the little brooks Mr. Dwelle
was able to have a small ditch run through his yard,
which supplied fresh, clear water for the stock.

Near by was the Madison river, which yielded him a bountiful supply of fish, while beyond was the forest, abounding in game of all kinds. The time until supper was spent in strolling around the ranch. In climbing one of the knolls near the house we discovered a grave, and upon a board which answered the purpose of a headstone was a simple inscription giving the man's name and the date of his death. When we returned to the cabin Mr. Dwelle was there with a large string of fish, which he proceeded at once to prepare for the table. While waiting for them to cook he told us the story of the lone grave on the hill. It was the last resting-place of a young Methodist minister, who had lost his health in his labors, and had come out to this country in the hope that the pure air would restore him to health. Like many others, he had put it off too long. He lived only three weeks, and during his sickness was taken care of by Mr. Dwelle, who, when he died, buried him on the most prominent knoll of the ranch. The mound is looked after by Mr. Dwelle, who has planted several bunches of beautiful mountain flowers upon it. Nearly everybody who stops at this place goes up to it and reads the inscription and desires Mr. Dwelle to give them the history of the green mound.

Supper being announced, we all responded to the call, and partook of one of the best meals we had eaten since leaving Portland. After doing full justice to it we returned to the reception-room, when several trappers came in and a very pleasant evening was spent listening to their stories

Taking an early start the next morning, we crossed the Madison river, which flows through the valley, and entered the forest. Most of the forenoon was spent in driving through miles and miles of dead timber, none of which appeared over ten inches in diameter. It had been destroyed by a forest fire which swept over this section some eight or ten years previously. In some places a new growth of pine and spruce was springing up, and, if another fire does not lay it waste, in a few years there will be quite a heavy growth of timber.

It was about noon when we crossed the boundary of the Yellowstone National Park and noticed for the first time soldiers of the Federal army doing police duty in preserving timber and keeping out trappers who sometimes get across the boundary in search of game. The road from this point to the top of the mountain is very heavy, as there is a great deal of sand

and no clay with which to build a solid road-bed. The mountains are undoubtedly of volcanic origin, as some of them are formed by a composition which has the appearance of slag.

Early in the afternoon we crossed the mountain and our eyes for the first time beheld " Wonderland." Vast columns of steam were ascending from the many geysers and boiling springs which abound in the valley. This section of the park was rarely if at all visited by Indians, who regarded it as the abode of the evil spirit.

Fording Firehole river we did not stop at the Lower Basin, but pushed forward to the Upper Basin, where we were to spend the night. On the way we passed the wonderful "Excelsior" geyser, whose crater is over three hundred feet in length and two hundred in breadth. Immense volumes of steam were issuing from it, and "Spikes," our driver, informed us that it had not been in eruption since 1888, and another disturbance was not due until 1894. It is said that while in action the quantity of water thrown out is so great that the Firehole river is raised several inches, and the water is so hot that no animal life can exist in it. This section is known as "Hell's Half Acre," from the great number of boiling springs in the vicinity.

Prismatic lake is perhaps a couple of hundred yards west from the "Excelsior," and receives its name from the many colors visible on its surface. The water in the centre of the lake is deep blue, gradually shading off to green. When the shallower portion of the lake is reached it assumes a yellow color, which deepens to a distinct orange. The formation around the rim of the basin is a brilliant red. The constantly rising volumes of steam are tinged with the colors that are so prominent in the pool, and form one of the most pleasing effects of the Park.

Going to the Upper Basin we were fortunate in reaching the "Grotto" geyser while it was in action. The cone of this geyser is the most peculiar of any in the Park. It has various cave like openings in the cone, and hence its name. While watching the jets of water and columns of steam issuing from the crater two ladies came up whom we recognized as having seen on the steamer we had met on our way to Alaska. In going up to the hotel we passed several of our original party which left Philadelphia on April 20th, and had been with us through all of our travels until we left them at Seattle, on our return from Alaska. We met them several times during our tour of the Park, and compared notes and experiences.

After eating our suppers we started out on a tour of inspection. Old Faithful was the first to secure our attention   This wonderful geyser gives an exhibition of its strength every sixty-five minutes with astonishing regularity. Through winter and summer, day and night, year in and year out, it is unerringly "on time." So regular are its eruptions that the name of "Old Faithful" is certainly no misnomer. Its eruptions begin with a few spasmodic spurts, which throw the water fully fifteen feet into the air. These are followed a few minutes later by a column of boiling water and steam several feet in diameter, which is thrown to a height of one hundred and fifty to two hundred and fifty feet. For several minutes this column remains, when it gradually recedes and lies dormant for sixty-five minutes. Then the phenomena is repeated.

It was late when we returned to the hotel, having spent several hours in walking over the formation and visiting the most important geysers. The Chinaman geyser received its name from the following circumstance : A Chinaman opened a laundry and pitched his tent over one of the boiling springs in order to have hot water convenient. After his first wash was finished he emptied the tub of soapsuds back into the

geyser, and the action of the alkali in the suds
started a violent commotion of the water in the
spring, followed by an explosion which threw
a column of water high into the air, carrying
away the tent and so frightening the Chinaman
that he disappeared, never to be seen again in
that vicinity. Since then, at irregular intervals,
the geyser becomes active and throws a column
of water about forty feet into the air.

It is said that this occurrence led to the discovery that soap thrown into any of the geysers will
produce an eruption almost immediately. The
soldiers keep constant watch upon the tourists to
prevent anything of the kind, but a few will
manage to "soap the geysers," notwithstanding.
"Spikes" said that some one had stolen the soap
from his room or he would have given us an example of its action on the water of one of the
most important geysers.

Desiring to make the Grand Cañon of the Yellowstone by evening, we left the hotel early in
the morning. Down past "Hell's Half Acre"
and the many boiling springs of the Lower Basin
we went, but did not stop, as we were to spend
the night there on our return. Fording a branch
of the Firehole river, we drove through a forest
of pine and spruce. Occasionally a number of

deer or elk would cross the road and disappear in the gloomy recesses of the forest. The road gradually narrowed and we entered the Gibbon Cañon. This rocky defile is about six miles in length, and in some places the cliffs are so close to the Gibbon river, which flows through the cañon, that there is scarcely room for the road. The Gibbon Falls is a beautiful cascade, and the rippling water coursing over the gentle incline forms a beautiful picture. On past the falls to the northward are numerous small springs with a strong sulphuric odor, some on one side of the river and some on the other. The only spring of importance is the "Beryl." It is one of the largest in the Park, and is quite near the roadside. The water is constantly boiling, and great quantities of hissing steam escape from it. The overflow from the rim of the spring runs across the roadway, and, although boiling hot, our horses did not hesitate an instant, but walked right through it.

It was about noon when we got the first sight of the Norris Basin of geysers. It is a barren tract, and resembles an immense area recently swept by a terrific fire. From many places jets of steam are constantly rising, and here and there are to be seen quite a number of geysers,

the most important of which are the Minute
Man, the Monarch, the Emerald, the Black
Growler and the Ink Well. The Minute Man
has an eruption every minute, and the water is
thrown about thirty feet into the air, although
some jets are thrown much higher. The Black
Growler is located quite near the road, on top of
the hill overlooking the entire basin. It takes
its name from the peculiar growling noise caused
by the great quantities of escaping steam and a
black deposit in the vicinity. It is what might
be called a steam geyser, as very little water is
discharged from its crater. The Ink Well is a
peculiar spring, about ten feet in width, and the
water, when at its lowest ebb, is about five feet
from the rim. The water gradually rises until
it gets almost rim-full, when it commences to
boil furiously and continues for about two or
three minutes. Then it will gradually recede
and fall to its lowest level, where it will remain
for a few moments, and then commence the exhibition anew. The air is heavily charged with
sulphur, and at several of the craters of the
steam-jets we got some very fine specimens of
pure sulphur. This basin is supposed to be of
more recent origin than any of the others in the

Park, as there is an absence of cones around the craters of the geysers.

The hotel having been burned, lunch was served in some tents which had been temporarily erected. The rest of the afternoon was spent in driving through forests of pine and fir. Along each side of the road were immense drifts of snow, and in some places they were fully ten feet deep.

It was about five o'clock in the afternoon when the stage pulled up at the Grand Cañon Hotel, where we were to stop while "doing" the wonders of this part of the Park. We had seen some of the beauties of the cañon as we drove along the road leading up to the hotel, and were anxious to see the rest before supper-time. After changing our dusty clothes for others clean and fresh, we started out for the cliffs overlooking the Yellowstone river. It is probably a quarter of a mile from the hotel to the trail that leads along the top of the cañon. As we emerged from a clump of trees the view of the many-colored cliffs and the green river thousands of feet below burst suddenly upon us. The combination of colors exceeded anything we had ever seen. The walls of the cañon had all the colors of the rainbow, but the predominating shade was yel-

low. There was the brilliant red and the duller
shades of the same color. There was the pure
white and the different shades of yellow so
blended that it was difficult to tell where one
commenced and the other ended. There was
the brown and the black, and the green and the
purple. In fact, the variety of colors was bewil-
dering. It is about two thousand feet from Inspiration Point to the bed of the Yellowstone
river. From this point one of the finest views of
the Grand Cañon is obtained, as it embraces the
Lower Falls of the Yellowstone and the delight·
ful exhibition of colors above described Along
the river's edge and up the sloping sides of the
cañon are numerous columns and pinnacles, all
painted with that indescribable conglomeration
of colors. Many of the loftiest ones have been
pre-empted by the eagles for their nests and the
rearing of their young, and the strange sight is
witnessed by those who walk along the trail
at the top of the cañon. There are many
of these noble birds here, and as they fly
up and down the cañon they look, in the
distance, like swallows skimming along through
the air. Near the trail is a large block of granite
known as the "Hague Boulder." It was evidently carried here during the glacial period, as
none of this kind of stone is found in this neigh-

borhood. We were late in returning to the hotel, but felt fully repaid for the five-mile walk we had taken. In the evening a number of us, in company with two soldiers who were stationed at this point in the Park, went to see the Upper Falls. We had to climb down over the rocks until we got on a projecting cliff directly in front of the falls, where the best view of the cataract is obtained, and were just far enough away to escape the mist which is constantly rising in clouds. So delighted were we that we must have remained there nearly an hour before we even thought of leaving. It was too late to go down to the Lower Falls when we reached the road, but as we had seen them in connection with the view from Inspiration Point, we thought that we had done up this portion of the Park quite thoroughly. On our return to the hotel we crossed the bridge over Cascade creek, a stream which joins the Yellowstone below the Upper Falls. This creek has its source in Mount Washburn, and at this point there are three beautiful little falls, known as the Crystal Cascades.

Leaving the Grand Cañon early in the morning we spent the entire forenoon in driving to the Norris Basin, where we again took luncheon in the tents. Leaving this point our faces were turned due north, and we were traveling to the most beautiful formations in the Park. The road is about the same as any other road through a forest. On either side are boiling springs, all of which have their names. Most of them are very clear, and the formations around the rims and on the sides are very beautiful. There are also numerous openings where nothing but steam issues forth. In these localities the odor of sulphur is also very strong. Roaring mountain is covered with these steam vents, and at times the quantity of escaping steam is so great that the roaring can be heard for several miles. It is from this peculiarity that the mountain takes its name Beaver lake is a body of clear water and receives its name from a colony of industrious little beavers that have built several dams across it and have their houses there. About ten miles from Norris Basin the road winds around the foot of the Obsidian Cliffs. This mountain stands by itself and is composed of volcanic glass. When the Indians were unskilled in the use of firearms this was known as neutral ground, and many of the tribes came here for their supply of arrow-heads. The United States engineers, in building this road, soon learned that blasting was impossible. They therefore built fires on the boulders and then dashed water on them. The sudden cooling of the mass caused them to break into many pieces, and in this manner the engineers constructed the only glass road in the world. Beyond the Obsidian Cliffs the road enters a declivity known as Swan Lake Basin. It is hemmed in on all sides by high mountains. In the winter great numbers of deer and elk make this their feeding-ground. Most of the high peaks have been given names. The highest one is Electric Peak. It was so named because the vast deposit of minerals in it renders the working of the surveyor's transit impossible when on the mountain.

About the middle of the afternoon we "rounded Cape Horn" and followed a road cut out of solid rock. As we neared the eastern end of it we passed through the " Golden Gate," so named from a pillar twelve or fifteen feet high which was left when the road was constructed and which forms a kind of gate-post. It is covered with a yellow moss, suggesting the name it bears. It was after four o'clock when we drove up to the Mammoth Hot Springs Hotel, where we were to stay for the night. In a short time guides were engaged and we started for the terraces formed by the deposits of carbonate of lime from the boiling springs issuing from the side of the mountain.

There are at least eight or ten well-defined terraces, which resemble immense bowls, arranged in groups, one above the other, at different places on the side of the mountain. Over the rims and sides of these basins trickles the hot water discharged from the springs, and it keeps ever fresh and sparkling the beautiful colors of the different basins. They are of all colors and are covered with particles which resemble diamonds. Every terrace has its name and all seem appropriate.

As one approaches them from the hotel the whole side of the mountain appears covered with beautiful basins of every color, from pure white to deep red and brown. Minerva Terrace was the first one visited. The basins and the formations in them vary in color from delicate cream to deep shades of red. It covers an area of over half an acre. In this spring many of the souvenirs of the Park are coated. Any hard substance placed where the water can run over it will in a few days become encrusted with crystal-like particles. Several men earn a livelihood in this way, as they have a monopoly of the business. Jupiter

Terrace, so named from being the largest on the mountain covers an area of about five acres. The spring which overflows this terrace is about one hundred feet in diameter. The coloring of the formations resemble those of the Minerva Terrace. Cleopatra's Terrace is the most beautiful of all. Its basins are pure white, and the boiling water, as it ripples down over the sides, seems studded with brilliant gems.

In most of the springs there appears along the edges a white, string-like substance known as "algea." It is a vegetable formation, and when the waters are quiet it spreads over the basins. According to some scientists it forms an important factor in producing the marvelous colorings that here abound.

Back from the terraces, and farther up the mountains, are several openings or small caves They have the euphonious names of "The Devil's Parlor," "The Devil's Kitchen," &c. They are extinct vents, and are entered with safety by many of the tourists. The Devil's Kitchen is entered by means of a ladder about thirty feet in length. As you descend, the air gets warmer, and the odor of sulphur is easily distinguished. On one side is a natural card-rack, and many persons have left their names

17

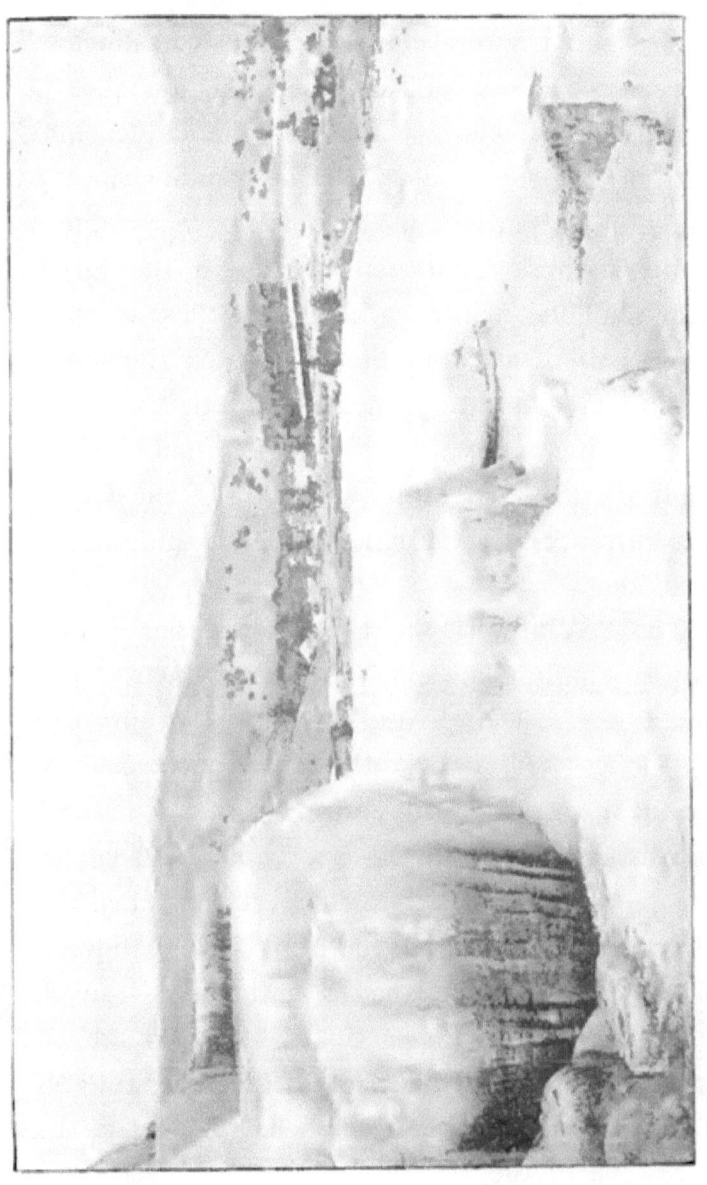

Minerva Terrace.

and addresses there. It is not many minutes before the perspiration starts and you have a desire to get out of the hole, and, as there is nothing to prevent, you climb the ladder and soon breathe the cool air. On reaching the top the guide informed us that some years ago a hunter, whose cabin still stands in the gulch near the hotel, while walking over these terraces saw a pair of antlers protruding above the snow, and upon examining them found that an elk, in roaming over the mountain, had broken through the crust of snow that had formed over the entrance to the kitchen and had hung there until dead.

The "White Elephant" is a peculiar formation resembling an elephant lying down. It is about ten feet high and probably seventy-five feet long. Of course all of the party had to mount it and walk the entire length. The head is a little lower than the body, and then comes the depression that forms the neck, and then the body. Extending from the head to the haunches along the centre of the formation is a row of sputtering hot springs. Sometimes they are all in action at once and at other times separately. This row of springs forms what is called the backbone of the elephant.

Following the trail that leads over the mountain past many springs which gush from its sides, we noticed that some appeared to be drying up, and that farther up the mountain are new springs. The guide informed us that this is continually happening—that the springs in this part of the mountain are finding outlets farther up the sides, and the lower openings are closing.

Passing over the Narrow Gauge Terrace, a formation much like the White Elephant, we again viewed the whole number of terraces, and as the setting sun beamed upon them they appeared brighter and if possible more beautiful than when we first beheld their dazzling colors. At the base of the terraces stands an extinct cone known as the Liberty Cap, about fifty feet in height and twenty feet in diameter at the base. It is some distance from the mountain, and from the appearance of the overlapping layers of carbonate of lime one would think it had no proper connection with the mountain. The Devil's Thumb is another of these cone-like formations, but it is imbedded in the side of the mountain.

As we approached the hotel the souvenir dealers attracted our attention, and we purchased a number of small articles to take away with us. The collection of specimens in the Park is beset with difficulties, as the soldiers are ever watchful, and you are politely informed that you must not take anything except what you buy at the stands.

In the morning we commenced to retrace our steps to Norris Basin, where we again took lunch in the tents, then proceeded through the Gibbon Cañon to the Lower Basin, where we spent our last night in the Park.

We were fortunate in arriving at the hotel when we did, as the manager informed us that the Fountain geyser would probably be active by the time we had finished our suppers. Nearly every one in the hotel was over at the pool very shortly after they had swallowed their last mouthful. It was some time before the violent action commenced, and while waiting we visited the mammoth Paint Pots near by. These "paint-pots" are large vats of boiling mud which are continually sputtering and throwing particles of mud in every direction. Some of the mud had a pinkish color and the rest shades off to pure white. Going back to the Fountain we made the acquaintance of one of the soldiers, who took us over the formation and showed us several beautiful springs which, had we been

alone, we should have missed.   One of these
was particularly interesting.   The water was
of an emerald hue, while the sides of the basin
were of the purest white.   In looking down into
the water we could see every formation that
would go to make up a fairy-bower.   There was
a general ripple on the surface which seemed to
impart life to all the recesses and the different
formations on the sides.   The sun was fast
setting behind the mountains that bound the
western confines of the Park, and the sky was
assuming an indescribable variety of tints peculiar to the western country.   The clouds were
all aglow with silver and crimson, and as they
moved along every color was faithfully reflected
upon the surface of the pool.

While watching for some indication of the
approaching eruption of the Fountain geyser, a
few bubbles were noticed coming up from the
depths of the pool, and then there was a lively
scampering to get out of the way of any stray
sprays of hot water that might reach the specta-
tors.   In a few moments the water shot up for
a distance of about twenty feet, which was
followed by one of those magnificent displays
of the workings of Nature which is only to be
witnessed in the Yellowstone Park.   We stood

for fully ten minutes watching the water as it was thrown to a height of from twenty to twenty-five feet, although sometimes jets would be forced to twice or three times that height.

In the morning we bade farewell to our friends with whom we had traveled across the continent and from Mexico to Alaska, and started for Beaver Cañon, where we were to take the Union Pacific railroad and proceed upon our homeward journey. Our friends who had entered "Wonderland" by the Northern Pacific route were to return to the Mammoth Hot Springs and from there to Cinnabar, where they would again enter the cars.

We would advise all who contemplate a visit to the Yellowstone National Park to enter one way and depart the other. It has become quite popular during the past few years to take the Union Pacific railroad to Beaver Cañon, and, taking the stages from that point, enter "Wonderland" at the southwestern corner, and after arriving at the Mammoth Hot Springs on the northern boundary to leave by going to Cinnabar, which is only nine miles from the Springs. This method prevents "doubling" on the way, and thus opens up a broader scope of territory.

Chapter VIII.

Homeward Bound.

ONLY two days were occupied in the return trip from the Lower Basin to Beaver Cañon. As we ascended the mountains that form the western boundary of "Wonderland," we looked back ever and anon until the road entered a depression and shut off our view of the rising steam from the many geysers and boiling springs of the valley.

When about half way down the mountain into the Madison valley we met several stages on their way to the park. Here we said good-bye to our driver, "Spikes," as he was to return with those going into the Park, and we were to have one of the younger drivers to conduct us back to the railroad. All morning we followed the meanderings of the Madison river, and at noon crossed it and drove up to Dwelle's cabin, where we were to take our dinner. He seemed pleased to greet us again, and cooked for the party an especial dinner, which consisted of fresh biscuits. antelope meat and mountain trout.

The whole afternoon was occupied in driving to Arangee Ranch. On the way over the Madison divide, through the Tvghee Pass, we saw the remnants of our picnic held there a week previous. The sun was just sinking below the mountains when we drove up to the cabins of Arangee Ranch, and we were again favored with one of those beautiful sunsets before spoken of.

The evening was passed in walking along the grassy banks of the familiar Snake river, until darkness drove us into the cabins. It was quite late when I retired, and consequently did not take much notice of the furniture of my room. On awaking in the morning the first thing to attract my attention was a coffin on one of the shelves on the side of the room. After breakfast we paid an exorbitant price for our accommodations and left. In crossing the Camas Meadows the mosquitoes were not so vicious as on our former visit, and we appreciated the fact very much. Our Yankee friend, it should be remarked, was continually popping away at birds and woodchucks, and always missing them. As we were ascending the last hill before entering Beaver Cañon I espied a Winchester rifle lying in the road, and, jumping down from the driver's boot, secured it. It now hangs on a nail in my bedroom, a trophy of my visit to the "Wonderland" of America.

It was after ten o'clock when we left Beaver Cañon for Salt Lake City, where we arrived about noon the next day. We put up at the Templeton Hotel, which is conducted by one of the sons of Brigham Young. It is located opposite the sacred square and the Lion House, once the abode of Brigham Young and his numerous wives. The Lion House is now the official residence of the president of the Mormon Church. Two days were spent in the sacred city of the Mormons, and while there we visited many of the points of interest in and around the city, including a trip to Garfield Beach, on the shores of Great Salt Lake.

Far up the sides of the mountain adjacent to the lake are to be seen the ancient shore lines. They are distinctly marked, and go to show that the whole valley now drained by the lake and its tributaries was once covered with water many hundred feet deep.

From here our objective point was Mount Carmel, in Illinois. Incidental stops were made at Pueblo, La Junta, Kansas City and St. Louis.

After a rest of a few days in the fertile valley of the Wabash we started for home, and in two days the familiar scenes of Pennsylvania and New Jersey greeted us, and we were HOME.

www.ingramcontent.com/pod-product-compliance
Lightning Source LLC
Chambersburg PA
CBHW031346020726
47499CB00005B/1418

* 9 7 8 3 7 4 4 6 7 0 7 7 7 *